VING CHILDREN A VOICE

by the same author

Street Wise
A Programme for Educating Young People about
Citizenship, Rights, Responsibilities and the Law
Sam Frankel
ISBN 978 1 84310 680 7
eISBN 978 1 84642 939 2

of related interest

Promoting Children's Rights in Social Work and Social Care
A Guide to Participatory Practice
Margaret Bell
ISBN 978 1 84310 607 4
eISBN 978 0 85700 486 4
Part of the *Children in Charge* series

Young Children's Rights
Exploring Beliefs, Principles and Practice
Second Edition
Priscilla Alderson
ISBN 978 1 84310 599 2
eISBN 978 1 84642 774 9
Part of the *Children in Charge* series

Helping Children to Tell About Sexual Abuse
Guidance for Helpers
Rosaleen McElvaney
ISBN 978 1 84905 712 7
eISBN 978 1 78450 235 5

Listening to Children
A Practitioner's Guide
Alison McLeod
ISBN 978 1 84310 549 7
eISBN 978 1 84642 784 8

GIVING CHILDREN
A VOICE

A Step-by-Step Guide to Promoting Child-Centred Practice

SAM FRANKEL

Jessica Kingsley *Publishers*
London and Philadelphia

First published in 2018
by Jessica Kingsley Publishers
73 Collier Street
London N1 9BE, UK
and
400 Market Street, Suite 400
Philadelphia, PA 19106, USA

www.jkp.com

Copyright © Sam Frankel 2018

The cover image is for illustrative purposes only,
and any person featuring is a model.

The resource sheets can be downloaded at
www.jkp.com/catalogue/book/9781785922787
for personal use with this program, but may not be reproduced for
any other purposes without the permission of the publisher.

Library of Congress Cataloging in Publication Data
A CIP catalog record for this book is available from the Library of Congress

British Library Cataloguing in Publication Data
A CIP catalogue record for this book is available from the British Library

ISBN 978 1 78592 278 7
eISBN 978 1 78450 578 3

Printed and bound in Great Britain

To Ruari, Rosie, Maria and Elsie

Would *adults* but generously snap our [children's] chains, and be content with rational fellowship instead of slavish obedience, they would find us…better citizens.

These words have been altered from the original written by Mary Wollstonecraft in her battle for women's rights in 1792 (Wollstonecraft 1792, p.104) and re-emphasised to reflect efforts today, which are no less revolutionary, to free the voice of the child.

CONTENTS

Acknowledgements   9

Getting Started: Creating a Culture of Advocacy .   11

PART 1: CREATING A CLIMATE FOR CHANGE . . .   23

1. Revitalise Your Thinking!   25

2. Be Spatially Aware   55

PART 2: TURNING RHETORIC INTO REALITY. . . .   83

3. Speak the Right Language   85

4. Creating Opportunities.   114

5. Lead the Change   139

Conclusion.   161

Resource Sheets   165

Useful Resources   177

Bibliography.   179

Index   183

ACKNOWLEDGEMENTS

This book would not have been written had it not been for two of my former students from Kings University College at the University of Western Ontario, Canada. Lindsay Izsac and Nadine Ivancovik are two dedicated young women who have demonstrated a deep and inspiring attitude to the importance of changing the way in which we, as adults, engage with children. They have been involved in this project from the start and, along with other students, their creativity and enthusiasm have been a massive influence on the content of this book. As well as the students, thanks also to staff on the Childhood and Social Institutions Programme at Kings, Sally McNamee, Alan Pomfret and Pat Ryan Kings, for the opportunities they created.

Thanks to Andrew James at Jessica Kingsley Publishers for taking on this project and his patience and guidance.

The ideas within this book very much reflect the evolving thinking taking place within EquippingKids. EquippingKids is an organisation that we have founded to create and make visible solutions that support children in navigating their everyday lives. Without, therefore, the input and ideas of my colleague John Fowler, this book would be without a backbone. John has not only read and re-read but directly inputed and shaped the journey of this writing project such that the text is littered with illustrations and suggestions that have grown out of our ongoing and exciting work with children.

Thanks to my team at home who put up with me writing – Ruari, Rosie, Maria, Elise and of course my wife Moira.

Finally, thank you to all those children that we work with who, through sharing their ideas, have demonstrated the reason why establishing a 'culture of advocacy' is so important.

GETTING STARTED
CREATING A CULTURE OF ADVOCACY

SECTION OBJECTIVES

For you to be clear on:

- the way in which advocacy is being defined – what is a 'culture of advocacy'?

- how children are to be positioned in relation to advocacy

- the framework to be used to help you create a culture of advocacy.

The aim of this book is simple. To provide you with a foundation through which you can establish a 'culture of advocacy' within your organisation, home or indeed any setting that you share with children.

A culture of advocacy is reflected in a setting in which:

- children's voices are acknowledged and valued

- opportunities are created to make sure that children's voices are heard.

Advocacy, in this context, is driven by the value that children's voices can bring to each and every setting that they experience, whether that is a home or school, a restaurant or courtroom, a playground or shopping mall.

By creating a culture of advocacy you will unlock children's potential to constructively contribute to the spaces that form part of their everyday lives.

A culture of advocacy sees adults and children working together to create shared spaces. It is relevant to adults whether they engage with children directly or indirectly, in formal or informal settings. A culture of advocacy moves beyond a traditional approach that is driven by adults speaking out for and on behalf of the child. Here children's voices are recognised for the contribution that they offer to improving practices and outcomes, as adults and children come together to positively transform key spaces within society, offering the opportunity to change their experiences and our experiences (as adults) too!

INTRODUCING ADVOCACY

Embracing a culture of advocacy can have a transformative impact.

Here are some quotes from children who were part of a pupil parliament in their primary school. They had been asked about the value of their parliament:

'I don't know how to explain it but it's a good opportunity to let me know that I have a voice.'

'You can say what you think and it can be in consideration for changes.'

'It helps everyone know how school is and helps make it more better.'

'It's a good thing because other children get to make ideas instead of the teachers having the ideas.'

'I think it is a good idea because if you're shy you get a turn to actually speak.'

The opportunity to have a voice is valuable. This book will suggest that, through encouraging children's participation and engagement, a culture of advocacy has positive implications both for the individual and for those many and varied community settings that children and adults share.

This book seeks to offer support to adults who are keen to pursue change through harnessing the potential of children's involvement and contributions. This book is not about demanding that only children have the answers. However, it does suggest that adults, alone, do not. To embrace that benefit and give transformation a real chance we need to create a new culture of advocacy, where opportunities for children to talk and be heard are both real and valued.

A desire to engage with children's voices changes the way in which spaces come to be experienced, wherever they may be. How we as adults come to recognise the possibilities of this, and the potential that it offers society, is an important challenge that we must engage with. For example, if we were better at hearing and acting on children's thoughts and ideas, how would that change the experience of going out for a 'family' meal, or of how children are positioned in formal legal settings, through to their place in schools and at home? A culture of advocacy offers a chance to create a truly shared space that is co-constructed and as a result is one where children experience a sense of purpose and belonging and which offers a basis for effective relationships and personal learning (in its broadest sense).

Each step that follows and the related 'actions' offer a guide to implementing a culture of advocacy. These ideas will allow you to test and evaluate a culture of advocacy in those settings where you engage with children and from this to build and shape a dynamic arena for interaction – full of potential benefits for both adults and children.

APPROACHING ADVOCACY

Are you an advocate for children?

'I am an advocate', wrote prolific English writer Sir John Mortimer (1998, p.59). Creator of the enduring character

Rumpole of the Bailey, Sir John Mortimer had good reason to call himself an advocate. He was a lawyer. Indeed his musings on the role of an advocate reflected the techniques and skills that might be used in the formal setting of a courtroom. At one point in his autobiography he highlights the extent to which the advocate becomes a go-between, an 'interpreter...between judges... and clients...in a reasonably short time I became bilingual and able to speak both "judge" and "client" and I formed a sort of glossary of useful phrases with their translations' (Mortimer 1998, p.111). It reflects a particular approach to advocacy. The advocate, who, through their training, is recognised as being best placed to represent the 'needs' and 'wants' of a particular group, taking their voice and re-configuring this for the ears of a decision-maker in a defined setting.

The example above offers a hierarchical model of advocacy, framed and shaped within the context of social institutions (here the legal system). It reflects a version of advocacy that illustrates the traditional way in which children have been positioned. Children here are the group whose 'needs' and 'wants' require translation and interpretation; their wants, as a result of some 'lack', are presented to the wider world of adults by a 'qualified' advocate. This advocate, thanks to specific training, is assumed to be able to understand the child and therefore offer an accepted version of the child's 'voice'.

However, should advocacy with children be based on little more than adults assuming their ability to effectively impersonate the voice of the child?

The purpose of this book is to question how we see advocacy and its relationship to children. This will mean questioning the role of the adult as advocate on behalf of the child. Indeed, as we explore that role further, it will become clear that adults do have a significant part to play in advocacy with children. This role might involve interpreting and translating, but it is more about creating opportunities, such that children have the confidence to share their voice in the first place, which may then lead to their further participation.

The point here is that adults are important. However, as we seek to engage with a culture of advocacy we need to recognise that it is not good enough to simply assume the voice of the child. In practice the experience and training of the adult needs to be driven more by a desire to unlock children's voices, as the adult as a facilitator creates platforms that allows the child to be heard. This book reflects the need for a true partnership where adults and children are able to combine knowledge, experience, perspectives and ideas in shaping the spaces that they share.

DEFINING ADVOCACY

Advocacy can certainly be put into the category of a 'contested concept' (Robinson 2015). It is one of those words that has a multitude of uses and meanings. It is, therefore, important to define how advocacy is going to be interpreted in this book as a first step in presenting a meaning that can have real application in the context of children's everyday lives.

Advocacy is of course:

- Martin Luther King Jr: 'I have a dream.'

- Nelson Mandela: 'Education is the most powerful weapon which you can use to change the world.'

- Barack Obama: 'Yes we can.'

But it is also the child who speaks out because they want an education or want others to know about the realities of their everyday life:

Dear friends, on 9 October 2012, the Taliban shot me on the left side of my forehead. They shot my friends, too. They thought that the bullets would silence us, but they failed. And out of that silence came thousands of voices. The terrorists thought they would change my aims and stop my ambitions. But nothing changed in my life except this: weakness, fear and hopelessness died. Strength, power and courage was born. (Malala Yousefzi, Speech to the UN General Assembly, 12 July, 2013)

I will always speak the truth. No one will shut me up even the whole world. (Bana Alabed, Tweet on 9 February, 2017)

The similarity that binds these examples together is that they represent one authentic voice which is being presented to other people. They reflect a call and offer the chance for others to respond. Each voice is being launched from a platform that allows others to hear it, whether in the courtroom, at a political rally, or through traditional news outlets or social media. So much of how we come to hear that voice is determined by our attitude towards it and the value we attach to it. The authentic nature of that voice is a defining catalyst for change. For ultimately change, whether large or small, starts with a voice.

The word advocacy is derived from the Latin, advoco, which means to call, invite, convoke or summon. Reflecting on that dictionary definition the notion of an offer to engage through coming together is particularly powerful. Advocacy, therefore, if we go back to the roots of the word, should not be separated from the idea of an individual or group 'calling out', as others are invited to share in matters of personal relevance and through their participation create the possibility of change.

Advocacy thus reflects a *stimulus* – the call – and a *response* – the opportunity to engage and participate.

We should be concerned with both stimulus and response in relation to creating a culture of advocacy with children. *This book seeks to connect advocacy, defined in terms of the passion and relevance of an authentic call, with children.* The *stimulus* is thus to be considered in terms of 'establishing the voice of the child', allowing them to find their voice. The *response* is about 'amplifying the voice of the child' and through this recognising the need for the creation of opportunities for children (and others) to engage and participate.

A culture of advocacy:

- establishes the child's voice: children's voices are acknowledged and valued

- amplifies the child's voice: opportunities are created that allow children's voices to be heard, giving others the chance to respond or engage.

Creating a culture of advocacy that values the voice of the child and gives children meaningful opportunities to respond as part of their everyday lives changes a pervasive dynamic of social interaction. Rather than children being merely the objects of adult concerns, children become partners, whose voices are not only openly heard and respected in their authentic state (without the need for an adult interpreter or guide), but whose participation is welcomed as a key ingredient for positive change and an embedded sense of shared communities in all the settings in which children live their lives.

DEFINING CHILDREN

It is important to be clear on the way in which children are viewed in this work. Consistently, children's place in advocacy has been as, at best, an observer. Traditional approaches to advocacy relate to children in terms of their developmental capacity. Here the aim is to move beyond this and to see children not in terms of their passivity but as active meaning makers, processing all that is going on around them (which influences their actions and reactions).

This does not need to get complicated and it will be explored in more detail in later sections, but what is being argued is that a traditional approach to the child looked like the following diagram (this is reflected in early models of the socialisation theory).

Here the child is merely a product of adult society. The contexts that adults provide, such as home and school, are there to mould the child. A 'normal' child will, through experiencing these contexts, become a 'normal adult'. At no point is it recognised that children will be making sense of these experiences themselves. Rather the child is seen as passive, there to be sculpted using the reliable tools of 'reward' and 'punishment'; their voice is of little value.

Arguably, one of the biggest changes in our thinking about the child in recent years has been to see a shift in the nature of that unidirectional arrow.

A bi-directional arrow recognises that children are not simply moulded by external forces; rather, children are processing what is going on around them as they make sense of the world they live in. As such children are creating meanings, meanings which have the power to shape the context itself. As soon as you recognise that there is a process, that children do not passively absorb what is going on around them but rather filter it, interpret it and then use it, then children's emotions, memories, experiences, sense of identity and, consequently, voice become of absolute relevance (based on ideas in Frankel 2017).

It is the active sense of the child, who is constantly processing what is taking place around them through the uniqueness of all that makes them 'them', that is the essence for how children are to be considered in all that follows. It is a way of thinking about the child that has developed under the banner of Childhood Studies. This is a multi-disciplinary approach that includes research in psychology, education, law, sociology, medicine and so on. It centres around the idea that children are social 'agents' – a term that reflects the extent to which they are responding to their social world and drawing off this as they shape meanings that come to inform their actions and reactions as well as their current and future ideas.

DEFINING THIS APPROACH

It is not without due regard to the enormity of the task that this book calls for a change in the way in which we approach advocacy with children. To help, the following chapters will rely on a framework that is currently being developed by EquippingKids and which is having an impact in schools in England (see Frankel and Fowler 2016). As we explore a culture of advocacy we will, therefore, draw on some of the tried and tested themes we are using in schools. Our school-based approach is, unsurprisingly, focused on children as learners. However, our definition of the learner is defined by recognising the social world that children are part of. A learner, therefore, is someone:

- growing in awareness of themselves and others
- developing knowledge and skills to navigate the social world around them
- maximising their potential through making the most of opportunities to participate and engage in the world around them.

The belief that learning is not an activity that should be restricted to the classroom pervades our approach in schools. Rather, it is a focus on those social or personal skills needed to maximise our effectiveness as lifelong learners that drives our work. However, this learning journey is limited unless it includes the chance for children to participate and engage in the world around them. This book, therefore, is focused on the third bullet point, as it seeks to draw out, through a focus on advocacy, the part that children can play as they develop their ability to get involved in the communities they are part of.

The following pages will, therefore, consider how we can create those opportunities for children to participate and engage. It will follow a model we are using in schools, linked to the wider themes of learning:

- Ethos – establish children as partners

- Community – design a space for the social learner

- Lead – champion a learning process

- Speak – compose a language for social engagement

- Act – initiate opportunities for practice.

As we now turn to building a culture of advocacy these steps have been adapted in order to promote a focus on children's voices and their wider social engagement. The steps are:

	Steps
Part 1: Creating a climate for change	Step 1 – Revitalise your thinking!
	Step 2 – Be spatially aware
Part 2: Turning rhetoric into reality	Step 3 – Speak the right language
	Step 4 – Create opportunities
	Step 5 – Lead the change

Each step is linked to a number of core 'actions' and 'reflections', both of which will help you to not only think about a culture of advocacy but to put it into practice!

Note: Each step will be supported by a number of actions, which will be introduced during these 'chapters'. You will need to interpret the steps and actions in the context of your work with your children. The aim here is not to provide you with all the answers, but rather to create a framework of actions that will put you in a strong position to engage with children to shape your own culture of advocacy.

Reflection

Having read this Introduction, what is it that you would like to achieve from reading the following pages? Where might you be heading on your journey? Why is such a journey necessary?

PART 1
CREATING A CLIMATE FOR CHANGE

Barack Obama, in his first public event since leaving the White House, said:

> what I'm convinced of is that although there are all kinds of issues I care about and all kinds of issues I intend to work on, the single-most important thing I can do is to help, in any way I can, prepare the next generation of leadership to take up the baton and take their own crack at changing the world. (Abc7 24 April 2017)

His message was clear: young people have significant potential. He went on to say:

> I have been encouraged everywhere I go in the United States – but also everywhere around the world – to see how sharp and astute and tolerant and thoughtful and entrepreneurial our young people are. So the question then becomes: What are the ways in which we can create pathways for them to take leadership, for them to get involved?

Of all he might do, following his time in the White House, Obama has recognised the power of engaging with children and young people, of impacting the future through creating opportunities 'today'.

Part 1 suggests that in creating such opportunities we need to free ourselves from the baggage that surrounds some dominant perceptions about the child. These perceptions have shaped and continue to shape and direct our understandings and the practices that we develop. If we are to create 'pathways to leadership' for children to 'get involved', then we need to detox ourselves from the passive views of children that limit and restrict the types of possibilities that are open to them.

We need to challenge our own thinking about children.

We need to challenge the thinking of others.

We need to recognise the value of children as partners.

REVITALISE YOUR THINKING!

Part 1: Creating a climate for change	Step 1 – Revitalise your thinking!	1. Recognise the noise
		2. Spot the assumption
		3. Your image of the child?
		4. Connect image and practice
		5. Notice their experience
		6. Refresh your image
		7. Imagine the difference
Section objectives	• To be able to reflect on what shapes our attitudes to children.
	• To understand and recognise the barriers that limit children's participation.
	• To increasingly see children as partners

Arguably the factor that most restricts children from establishing a voice and having platforms through which that voice can be amplified is us, adults!

If we are the issue, then it is with us that we must begin to search for a solution.

To rile you or make you defensive is not the purpose of this challenge. But it is a challenge nonetheless. For, however long we have worked with children, whatever our qualifications or experience, it is vital that we give ourselves the time to reflect on how we think about children. Why? For the simple reason that, irrespective of how progressive our views on children are, we are living in a world that is dominated by opinions about children that are incomplete. Incomplete because these views have for too long been based on what adults think about children, rather than balancing that with what children think too!

Prince William created headlines in April 2017 by saying that the British stiff upper lip should be replaced by people talking openly about their emotions. Notably, this included children. In an interview with one charity magazine the Prince said, 'Catherine and I are clear we want both George and Charlotte to grow up feeling able to talk about their emotions and feelings.' He went on, 'Over the past year we have visited a number of schools together where we have been amazed listening to children talk about some quite difficult subjects in a clear and emotionally articulate way, something most adults would struggle with' (*CALMzine* 2017).

It is notable that in 2017 headlines can be created by someone saying that they hope that their children will grow up talking about their emotions, and that there is surprise over the fact that children do this already!

Our thinking about children and a set belief that they are not capable of engaging with their emotions has dominated for millennia. We should be encouraged that these views are being challenged, but that such challenges need to be made in the first place shows how far we still have to go.

To establish a culture of advocacy and to improve our capacity as individuals to engage with children effectively it is important for us to go through a process of regular detox as we draw out all those invasive attitudes about children that can limit our engagement and restrict effective practice. This chapter will take you on a journey of detoxification and revitalisation (one you can make personal use of, or share with others).

DETOXING OUR VIEW OF THE CHILD

A traditional detox programme might encourage you to think about what you eat and drink and the amount of exercise or rest you have; this detox programme is going to be slightly more cerebral than that, as we look to take on what is in our heads, perhaps extracting unwanted ideas and engaging new ones or simply refreshing connections and dusting off a memory that has been locked away. Despite this being a mental exercise, that does not mean we can't make it practical (see the Reflections at the end of each step)!

Detox

Action 1: Recognise the noise

Action 2: Spot the assumption

Action 3: Your image of the child?

Action 4: Connect image and practice

Action 5: Notice their experience

Revitalise

Action 6: Refresh your image

Action 7: Imagine the difference

ACTION 1: RECOGNISE THE NOISE

Our thinking about children is influenced by the multitude of views and ideas that are present all around us.

'My mum always said…'

'In the news that child was…'

'In my training children were described as...'

'Those children at the bus stop...'

These different views on children come to inform a backdrop, which in turn becomes the scenery in front of which we interact with children.

It would be a hard task to define all the sources of the 'noise' that come to inform our views on children. Although, as a first step in raising our awareness of the 'noise', it is helpful to have some sense of where that noise might come from.

Defining the Noise

Views informed by:	As seen through:	Examples
The space we are in	• The country, town, community we are in • The current political climate	Political initiatives focused on school-starting age (note the variations even within Europe)
Cultural traditions	• Our customs and conventions • Religious practices	Approaches to parenting
Formal practices	• The law • Defined (institutional) policies	Ages at which the law defines individual responsibility
Popular trends	• The media • Themes in literature or in films • The internet • Consumer patterns	Presentation of children in the news
Our legacy	• History (philosophical thought, institutional metholologies)	Theories that reflect on when children are 'ready' to take part in 'reasoned' thought

'Noise' about children is all around us. As individuals, what we come into contact with and what we are influenced by will differ; for this first step we simply need to be aware of the noise itself.

Reflection

To be able to detox, we first need to heighten our awareness of the noise and visually reflect on the backdrop in front of which our interactions with children take place.

1. With Resource Sheet 1 in front of you, use the headings above and see what 'noise about children' you are aware of. Write these onto the sheet.

Note: Without even knowing it you will automatically be exploring noise that is relevant to the settings where you engage with children. As the process continues, it is important to recognise that different settings will be influenced by different noises, which in turn will lead to different experiences for children.

2. You may want to prioritise the noise. Is some noise more 'noisy'?

3. If undertaking this activity with a group, it works well if you first have a go on your own and then contrast your thoughts with other members of the group.

ACTION 2: SPOT THE ASSUMPTION

Fake news is a hot topic at the moment.

The obvious problem with fake news is that information gets presented as fact, when it is not, and this is then accepted by an audience. The attitude of the audience is then influenced by what they have heard. Increasingly, companies are setting up services to spot that fake news.

In many ways, the example of fake news acts as an illustration for the way in which certain views about children have been presented and re-presented by adults over millennia. This noise about children has identified particular understandings about children, which have been accepted as accurate by a generally undiscerning adult audience. Views which are not accurate have shaped and continue to shape how we think about children.

Action 2, therefore, is that we develop our ability to spot the 'fake news' in relation to children.

Much of the noise that we identified in Action 1 is based on a number of assumptions about children. These assumptions have influenced, and continue to significantly influence, a hier-archical relationship between adults and children. Below, I have identified three recurring assumptions.

- The universal child

- The future child

- The protected child.

These assumptions pop up regularly in the 'noise' surrounding children. They act as barriers to children's participation and engagement and have limited the extent to which children's voices have been, and are, valued. If we are to create an effective culture of advocacy we need to be able to spot these assumptions. It is therefore helpful to know a little more about them and how the struggle/quest for children to be heard is connected with the efforts of other marginalised groups to have *their* voices heard.

The universal child

The assumption: All children are the same.

The fact is that this view has dominated our approach to children for a very long time.

One of the features that has allowed children to be 'universalised', to be seen as one group, is their age. Children can do nothing about their age. What *can* change is the way in which adults think about it. Too often because of their age, children find themselves marked out, defined, categorised and stamped as 'children'. Once labelled it then becomes easy for other assumptions (some of which follow) to then be attached to the child.

When children are viewed as a universal group it is simple for adult assumptions to be transferred from one child to the next, making it easy for adults to manage children. The most obvious example of this is compulsory schooling. It reflects a system where what is seen as right for one 7-year-old is also seen as right for all other 7-year-olds. However, the education system is not alone, children's experiences within the legal system (age of criminal responsibility), health care (decisions on treatment) and welfare, reflect further examples where society has for too long been focused on responding to children as one group, rather than seeing them as individuals.

CASE STUDY: Children in the legal system

A very obvious example of the universal child is the way in which ages are defined within the law.

One example is the age of criminal responsibility. What is interesting about this, is that not only is it set at an age, suggesting all children will reach this moment of knowledge at exactly the same time, but that this time of enlightenment is different depending on where you live. Even in Europe, there is considerable difference from the age set in England and Wales, where a child is criminally responsible at 10 years, and other countries, for example:

- Belgium – 12 years
- Denmark – 15 years

- Germany – 14 years
- Spain – 14 years
- Turkey – 12 years.

The arbitrary nature of ages within the law is also reflected by the way the civil law attaches behaviours to ages. For example, in England and Wales:

- at age 16 you can consent to sexual intercourse, buy aerosol paint, buy a lottery ticket
- at age 18 you can vote, buy alcohol, bet in a betting shop, get a tattoo.

This contrast is so effectively summed up in the following quote:

> On the one hand, then there is a denial of children as rational responsible persons able to receive information, participate in frank and open discussions and come to well reasoned and appropriately informed decisions about their interpersonal relationships (family, friends, sexual), about school and developing sexuality. On the other hand there is the imposition, using the full force of law, of the highest level of rationality and responsibility on children and young people that seriously offend. The paradox is that the same sources appear to propose that childhood represents a period of diminished adult responsibility governing certain actions while being a period of equal responsibility governing others. (Scraton 1997, p.182)

What is significant about regarding children as a universal group is that it has been used to deny children a voice (the voice of the individual is of little relevance if all children are to be viewed as the same). What emerges from the following historical example shows a connection between efforts to universalise a group with one hand and suppress their voices with the other.

If a culture of advocacy with children is going to be effective then we need to recognise children as individuals.

THE ROBIN HOOD EFFECT

The story of Robin Hood illustrates the value of recognising the individual in the face of a more powerful group who, to suit their own ends, are happy to 'universalise' the other. But more of Robin Hood later.

What we have seen above is that it is easy for children to be lumped together. It is very easy for societies to simply label children in terms of their childishness and, as a result, to respond to all children as a universal group.

Of course, the argument here is that this universalisation of certain groups in society has a disabling impact on voice. Not only does the voice of the individual go unheard, it is not even recognised in the first place.

The challenge, therefore, is to find a way to recognise the individual. It is a battle in which managing power has always been a key feature, and it is well summed up in the following quote:

> It is worth bearing in mind that the vulnerability of children derives, in some part, not from their lack of capacity, but rather, from their lack of power and status with which to exercise their rights and challenge abuse. (Lansdown 2010, p.19)

Indeed it is not misleading to suggest that in the past the voices of the many have been 'owned' by those with greater power. Stretching all the way back to the Classical period we can see that the voice that was valued was the one that was wealthy, male and had recognised lineage.

The voice of the individual on a day-to-day basis thus went unheard and unacknowledged.

So where does Robin Hood fit into all of this? Well, Robin Hood and his band of merry men may just have been English legend, or not, but the enduring nature of this story, which surfaced in England in the 1300s, reflects a challenge to that traditional power. The story shows, through ballads and writings, how Robin Hood became a focus through which to challenge the universalisation of the poor by raising the plight of the individual. The tales of Robin Hood challenged the hierarchy of English society by attaching value to the unseen and unheard peasant classes.

That same idea is reflected in other stories from other times and taps into a wider consciousness that each person, no matter what their background, is to be valued.

English history is littered with examples from the last 1000 years (alone) in which those with power have been challenged to recognise the individual. From the Magna Carta (and the fettering of the monarch's power) to putting books, like the Bible, into a common language (such that more people could understand and interpret them), to growing political representation, slowly the individual has been recognised and the position of the powerful has been made more accountable.

Indeed, it was a fight for the place of the individual that informed the philosophical revolution of the 1600s and beyond, where ideas about the individual literally shaped the world. Thomas Hobbes, John Locke and Thomas Paine were just three men whose pens were driven by efforts to rebalance power and to ensure that the value of one's voice was not represented by the weight of one's purse.

John Locke, for example, arguably shaped the American Declaration of Independence and the Bill of Rights and Thomas Paine's ideas shook those on both sides of the Atlantic. Indeed, his book the *Rights of Man* (1791) was the most widely read book of the day. The second American President, John Adams said of Paine, 'without the pen of Thomas Paine, the sword of Washington would have been wielded in vain'.

Washington's sword, of course, was wielded to offer a different system of governance where the individual was not simply one of many, and for those who were part of the newly constituted USA there was a sense of shared value (highlighted in the famous opening words of the Declaration of Independence – 'We hold these truths to be self evident: that all men are created equal'). Indeed, as we jump forward, it was such changes that moved us to a point internationally where there is now a shared statement on the human rights of the individual. It is the ultimate recognition of the value of the individual.

Despite progress, today we continue to universalise groups in society, which has a negative impact on our ability to hear their voices. This is the case for none more so than children. What this historical reflection shows is that the fight for the voices of individuals to be valued has been long fought. It is that battle, however, that we must keep fighting as we seek to free the individual child so that their voice can be heard.

The future child

The assumption: Children's value lies in what they will become.

We have seen that universality is a feature of the way in which we have come to construct an image of the child, so too is competence. Competence, as we shall see, has been effectively used to suppress or deny the voice of the individual. This has been the case not only in relation to children but also with many other groups. Of course if the competence of an individual can be denied or questioned then this automatically undermines the value of their voice.

For children, competence has been defined by the ages and stages in their lives. This developmental approach assigns children of a certain age to a list of abilities (physical and mental). Notably this has included assessments of children's ability to 'reason' and thus their capacity to be capable of offering a meaningful view on a given subject. For example, developmental theories have seen the age of 12 years set as the moment when children were 'ready' to engage (for example, the influential work of Jean Piaget), as it was only at this point that their mental faculties allowed for effective participation.

Assigning a level of competence to a particular stage in the life course means that the child's only real value (in terms of effective participation and the relevance of voice) is defined in terms of what they might be in the future.

To ensure that children are seen as partners we need to challenge this and to recognise the importance of children's competence both today and for tomorrow.

A MINORITY REPORT

A feature of advocacy (and the value of the individual voice) has been the way in which narratives on 'competence' have been used by some to maintain power over others.

Engaging with minority status, whether in relation to women, black and ethnic groups or indeed children, one becomes aware of the extent to which powerful cultivated discourses were designed to shut out the voices of individuals from these groups, maintaining the status quo through protecting their position.

A couple of historical examples illustrate how competence has been used as a tool to discredit the voice of individuals from certain groups.

Olaudah Equiano was an advocate. Not in a formal sense, he was not a lawyer, rather he was a spokesperson. In 1789, after a few years in London, he wrote his autobiography, drawing on his own experiences to challenge slavery. He says of the transatlantic trade that it 'violates that first natural right of mankind, equality and independency, and gives one man a dominion over his fellows which God could never intend' (1789, p.109). Slavery was based on the simple assumption that one group had natural superiority over another. Equiano reflected that it was:

> necessary to keep them [slaves] in a state of ignorance; and yet you assert that they are incapable of learning, that their minds are such a barren soil or moor, that culture would be lost on them; and that they came from a climate where nature has left

men alone scant and unfinished, and incapable of enjoying the treasures she has poured out for him. (1789, p.110)

A natural inferiority, fuelled and directed by assumptions, becomes a key feature, therefore, of the justification that the 'powerful' use in order to maintain their position of control over the minority. For Equiano it was not until 'slaves were seen as men', as equals, as partners in the social world, that 'peace, prosperity and happiness' (1789, p.111) would result. It was only when one group saw beyond the assumptions of the other that change would really take place.

Similar arguments are present in the powerful words of another change maker, Mary Wollstonecraft, who advocated for society to re-address the way in which it thought about women. Women, like slaves, were seen consistently through assumptions about competence. Wollstonecraft writes of how:

> the minds of women are enfeebled by false refinement…they are treated as a kind of subordinate beings, and not as part of the human species, when improvable reason is allowed to be the dignified distinction which raises men above creation and puts a natural sceptre into a feeble hand. (Wollstonecraft [1792] 2004, p.2)

Indeed she goes on to highlight at the start of her influential book, A Vindication of the Rights of Women (1792), how being a woman limits how one is 'heard' and, therefore, she argues, this must be addressed. Constant themes of power pervade, as Wollstonecraft seeks to establish women's voices as 'of value' and 'as competent', in order to create an accepted foundation from which they can be heard.

For Wollstonecraft, men's categorisation of women as inferior all came down to their ability to 'reason'. Indeed, it was that perceived lack of reason that seemingly put women in a separate category to men. It is the pervasive acceptance of this lack of competence held by individuals and knitted into the very fabric of society that she saw as fatally undermining the value of women's voices.

This attitude towards women had implications for women's experiences. In relation to domestic violence, groundbreaking team Dobash and Dobash write:

> they [Rousseau, Hegel, Kant, Fichte, Blackstone, St Augustine, John Knox, Calvin, Martin Luther] believed that men had the right to dominate and control women and that women were by their nature subservient to men. This relationship was deemed natural, sacred, unproblematic and such beliefs resulted in long periods of disregard or denial of the husband's abuses of his economic, political and physical power. (Dobash and Dobash 1992, p.7)

A way of thinking based on attitudes which held that women were by nature inferior to men ensured the domination of women. It is only in recent history that this has really begun to change. Indeed, it is only in the last 50 years that, as a result of women breaking these assumptions, that horrors like domestic violence have become visible within society. 'In 1971, almost no-one had heard of battered women...many people did not believe such behaviour actually existed' (Dobash and Dobash, 1979, p.2). This battle to change attitudes to domestic violence therefore began with 500 women, some children and a cow, from a small English village, who initially were campaigning to protect free milk in schools. Notably, unbeknownst to them at that time, this local group were starting a movement that was going to have an impact around the world. A realisation of common interests kept the group together. They started to talk – as they realised that *their* voice was valued. Meeting gave them a forum and a growing opportunity for their voices to be heard as they spoke to one another about the oppression that they faced on a day to day basis, which collectively evolved into a project for change. Despite some progress, that fight for women to be free from domestic violence is still plagued by themes of inferiority, as men seek to defend their actions by asserting an invented sense of greater competence.

Practices influenced by a view or image of women as lacking competence were not just confined to the home but can be seen in society as a whole. Voting rights offers a good illustration. Indeed nineteenth-century history is littered with international examples of men, without exception, being granted the right to vote. Women did follow, but it took more time. One example that highlights the issues facing minorities is that Canadian women were given the right to vote in 1917 but, notably, it was not until 1960 that this came to include aboriginal women too.

The 'de-competencing' of certain groups in society, in order that the powerful might protect and maintain their position, has a significant history. For children today, the issue of competence is an easy tool for adults to wield in order to exclude children's voices. However, as we have seen, assumptions about competence and inferiority reflect methods used for muting or silencing certain groups. If we are to create a culture of advocacy, if children are to become partners, then we need to recognise and challenge such assumptions.

The protected child

Assumption: Adults always know best!

Within society we seem to simply accept that adults are imbued with an automatic ability to know what is in a child's best interests.

The United Nations Convention on the Rights of the Child (UNCRC) 1989, which has become the most signed international convention, was a great move for children. Wasn't it? The Convention highlights the issues that we face as we seek to position children's voices in society. Yes, of course there are some very positive elements that stem from the UNCRC, however the question is who controls this. Who is it that has the power to inform children of the convention in the first place? Who is it that acts as a gatekeeper to children accessing their rights? Indeed, who wrote the convention and defined the rights that it contained? The answer is of course 'adults'. So much of our thinking in relation to children has been dominated by the role that adults come to play in relation to children. This role has positioned adults as decision-makers for children, as the directors of their lives.

A key part of our efforts to change the way in which we view advocacy lies in the need for us to move away from a best interests model, in which adults define the 'best interest', to one in which adults and children arrive at a conclusion together. It is important to note that the aim is not to deny the role that adults play in providing protection. However, what it does invite us to do is to put our approach to protection into a wider context, where opportunities can be created for children to become part of a dialogue on 'their' best interests.

ADULTS TO THE RESCUE

As we have seen above, a key feature of the noise surrounding children has been defined by themes of universalisation and an assessment of the child's 'lack' of competence. This section reflects on a period in which it was increasingly seen as a 'worthy' act to advocate for children, as adults assumed that they had all the answers.

The 1800s saw significant social change. This change meant that not only were there more children, but that these children were more visible to the middle classes. Selfishly, many only saw the threat it posed to them, both in relation to their pockets, (the money they might be asked for to respond to an impoverished underclass within their parish) to their property and person (as fears grew both of social disruption and increased levels of crime). However, others began to see the dangers of children working in factories or having to live out on the streets. Increasingly there were children who needed to be 'rescued'.

It was, however, in response to a strong developmental understanding of the child, in which the child was constrained within their unformed, feeble and suggestible body that society looked to take more responsibility for 'protecting' the child and 'providing' for them. From emerging organisations such as Barnardo's to the NSPCC and the Children's Society, the focus was on adults interpreting the problem and coming up with their solution.

It was this adult-centric formula that became the basis for the approach to children and advocacy in the twentieth century. Two examples of adults thinking they knew best have already been mentioned, compulsory schooling and children's rights. As well as these, many government policies have taken it upon themselves to impose a 'childhood' that they consider 'best'. A striking example of where such an approach resulted in a catastrophic mistake was the efforts of governments in Canada and Australia to remove aboriginal children from their communities and to impose on them a particular education that was driven by a desire to create a common childhood experience (explored more on page 77). At no point was this process informed by the families of the children or the children themselves. Their voices were of no value in defining what the expectations were in terms of these children's need for protection and provision. It is a policy that has caused major social issues.

Advocacy here is defined by 'qualified' adults speaking out for the 'unqualified' child (and their family). The noise on children has thus been dominated by adult assumptions rather than a sense of the value in speaking to or engaging with the child themselves.

The journey of thinking and action above has left a definite legacy in which it is assumed that children are not a necessary ingredient to creating change. However, as we will argue, it is only through children's *participation* that protection and provision can really be effectively addressed.

Note: These three sections simply reflect some dominant assumptions that continue to influence how we think about children and approach advocacy with them.

Reflection

1. Take the noises you identified in the previous reflection and using the three headings above see if you can recognise any aspect of these assumptions within that noise.

2. Can you recognise any other assumptions that are attached to the noise you identified?

Note: As you start to connect the noise and assumptions to a particular setting where you interact with children, you can begin to reflect more directly on the specific noise and assumptions that come to influence the spaces where you engage with children and which can be written into the 'roof' space on Resource Sheet 1 (Action 3 will explore this further).

ACTION 3: YOUR IMAGE OF THE CHILD?

These elements of noise come to inform an image of the child that we hold.

An image of the child here refers to a personal understanding of the child, which then comes to inform our thoughts and actions. We all do this. These subconscious images give us a shortcut to creating meanings that help us make sense of children and give us a basis for the practices we use with them. Our images will be linked to particular settings where we interact with children. As such, in our heads we will often have a range of 'images' that we can then employ; an image of children in school will be separate to an image of the child at home or in the playground.

The challenge for us is that because these images are intended to inform a short cut they rely heavily on easy to gather information, such as those assumptions that are most prominent in the noise about children that surrounds us. That said, these images are not fixed and they can change!

Here are some features of the image of the child that are worth thinking about. An image of the child:

- is constructed – as we draw on that noise about children

- will be linked to those different settings where we interact with children

- shapes how we think and act – our practices and the language we use (Action 4)

- (and ultimately) will define children's experiences (Action 5)

- can change (Actions 6 and 7)!

Each of these points interlinks but they can also stand alone. Indeed, they all relate in some way to the different steps in this book.

An image

As we have suggested, 'noise' about the child surrounds us.
We are therefore exposed to that noise and related assumptions.
We will draw from that noise to frame our image of the child.

At times in society some of that noise might get particularly loud. There is, therefore, greater chance that this will impact on the image of the child that we hold.

An ongoing example of this is in relation to children and crime. Across generations we can see spikes at certain times when the behaviour of young people comes in for particular attention. The noise increases. As a result the way people view the child, their image of the child, alters. This is reflected in increased fear, a more determined attitude towards punishment and so on.

The internet provides another example of a situation in which adults are being surrounded by particular noise about the child. This noise will impact on the image we have of the child, such as:

- my child will be easily influenced

- screen time has a negative impact

- my child is vulnerable to exploitation.

The image we hold will then be played out in the practices we use to allow (or not) children's use of the internet.

CASE STUDY

A newspaper report in 2014 highlighted a number of these themes. It was titled 'from hoodies to goodies'.[1] It focused in on a report that showed how children wanted to be involved in society, how they were passionate about doing good. However, this was in contrast to 'images' of the child that adults had, images that were connected to assumption about children's antisocial behaviour and their egotistical view of life. We all hold images of the child, the question is – are they the right ones?

Another interesting example that plays with this notion of image is seen on a short video 'Let's save Africa'.[2] It highlights the way in which charities have sought to reinforce a particular image in order to communicate a message. The issue is that this image of the vulnerable 'African' child (in the context of this clip) has become

---

1   www.theguardian.com/commentisfree/2014/feb/16/hoodies-goodies-teenagers-makings-good-citizens-young

2   www.youtube.com/watch?v=xbqA6o8_WC0

dominant and in most cases does not reflect the reality of children's lives. Another image is needed.

Reflection

1. Pick a setting in which you engage with children.

2. Prioritise the noise (Action 1) and the assumptions (Action 2) that you feel are particularly relevant in that setting (these can be entered into the image in the roof space of Resource Sheet 1).

3. Then consider which bits of noise (and the assumptions connected to them) inform your view of the child in this setting and how these combine to create a particular image of the child.

4. Now try this exercise again. Pick a different setting – how does your image of the child change?

ACTION 4: CONNECT IMAGE AND PRACTICE

Our 'image of the child' will impact on how we engage with children.

It is as simple as that. The image of the child that we have will shape the nature of our actions towards them. These actions may take form in the context of policies or processes that we might write or set out in the 'cool light of day' as well as in our actions or reactions in the 'heat of the moment'. Our image of the child will define what options we see as available to us for engaging with children. For example, a particular 'image' might shape a parent's inclination to use, or not, a 'naughty step' or 'confiscation' as part of managing children's behaviours (for more on contrasting parenting styles, see Kohn 2005), through to the way in which we communicate with children our feelings about a situation (from the adult who shouts to the adult who explains).

Making this connection between the image we hold and the practices we use is so important. If we recognise that what we do is driven by how we think about children, then we are better placed to recognise how, if needed, we can change that cycle – so that, along with our change in attitude, there is also a change in practice.

Reflection

Use Resource Sheet 1 to consider the link between your image of the child and the practices that you use. Explore this in different settings.

Analysing the practice of others

The actions within Step 1 can be used to analyse the practice of others.

However, unlike our own personal detox, if we are 'looking in' on a situation we will often find that we start with practice and then have to work backwards (as well as forwards).

Often, in the context of using this model to problem-solve a particular interaction between adults and children, it can be easier to start with the practice. As we examine 'practice', therefore, we are looking to identify particular actions, activities, processes or policies that are being used. Here is an example:

The Scenario: Harry and his brother were going to bed on a Friday night. They were laughing and in high spirits, although they were both trying to keep the noise down as they knew their neighbours might be able to hear. Their dad thought they were being too loud. So...

Practice: Dad shouted at them. He was physically aggressive. He would not listen to their side of the story and sent them straight to bed.

If we want to effectively challenge the way in which the dad acted, it is important to have some understanding of the way he thinks about children. His practices give us a clue; the next step though would be to work with the dad to establish a sense of his 'image' of the child. This would provide an opportunity to consider how his approach to parenting draws on some traditional assumptions about hierarchy, control, and the use of reward and punishment.

By raising awareness of the noise, the assumptions and the image that we hold, we can then start to challenge our own practices.

ACTION 5: NOTICE THEIR EXPERIENCE

As was suggested in the Introduction to this book, children are far from passive. This means that the way we engage with children and the practices that we follow have an impact on their experience.

In the previous section an example was shared of a dad trying to get his children to bed. What follows is an extract where one of the children involved reflects on the practices that their dad used.

> **Harry:** I don't think my dad should have been that angry because it was a Friday night and we weren't doing anything the next day and it wasn't that late, it was only about half past eight, so I think we should have been able to stay up a little bit longer, and it's because we've got babies and toddlers living next door, we weren't being that loud either, we were just laughing loudly sometimes but we weren't laughing that loud.

Harry could not understand why his dad was so angry when he had considered not only the level of noise but the time of night and the day of the week. So why had his dad reacted in this explosive way?

For Harry, this experience left him confused. However the actions of the dad (his practices) could have created a very different experience. For example, had the dad engaged with Harry and helped him to explore whether the choices he had made were the 'right' ones – Harry might have been left with an experience that offered answers rather than leaving questions.

It is important for us to be aware that whatever the practices that we employ they will impact on children's experiences. Children will reflect on the practice and they will process this and this will impact on what they think. The key is that we can make those experiences positive.

CASE STUDY: Was that fair?

One of the regular questions children ask in relation to adult practices in schools is 'was that fair?' Fairness can easily emerge as the result of a power relationship. It is, and has been, a theme in the battle that groups have had in order to find their voice. That question of fairness can be managed by adults recognising that their actions do impact on children's experiences.

Here two boys are reflecting on their head teacher:

Nat: I think Miss Phillips [the head teacher] is quite good at sorting out problems. Because I did a trade the other day with my friend, my sort of friend Robert, and all of a sudden he said he wanted to trade back and I didn't want to and so Miss [a member of staff on the playground] couldn't sort it out so we went to Miss Phillips. Miss Phillips always has a sensible way to sort out, the fair way. She listened to both sides of the story and she made us trade back but now Robert's not allowed to bring his cards in so I got an unfair part and Robert got an unfair part.

Josh: Nathan, remember when you were like really, really, really like annoying me and intimidating me in the playground last year?

Nat: Yeah, I had to run away from you.

Josh: I ran and I jumped and you cut your knee so badly.

Nat: It was funny.

Josh: And we went to Miss Phillips and she just sat us down and said 'what's the problem?' She listened to both sides of the story, exactly the same as that, and she gave us both a fair thing that we stay away from each other. But now we've made up. (Frankel 2012, p.165)

The importance of recognising that children will process and make sense of the practices we use is so important as it encourages us to think about the experience it creates.

Reflection

Continue to add to the previous reflection. How might your practices impact on children's experiences? Considering how children experience these practices is relevant whether their reflections are positive or negative.

Remember the most effective way of assessing how children experience practices is by asking them!

Now you have drawn out some of those 'toxic' notions about the child, it is time to revitalise the system.

ACTION 6: REFRESH YOUR IMAGE

There is 'noise' about children that can be drawn on to shape a more positive image of the child. Noise that is not tainted by limiting assumptions. Here are some examples (with more to explore in the 'Useful Resources' at the end of the book):

A. Universal Child to Individual Child

A change in academic and popular attitudes towards the child in the 1970s started to pave the way for the individual child.

Key to this was a growing recognition that children were not passive products of society but actively making meanings as they processed what was going on around them. Research was reflecting that children's reactions were not universal, they were personal.

As well as this being picked up by academics, it was being reflected in other areas too. One example of this was in the courts. In a case (Gillick v West Norfolk HA) that had a significant impact on the 'image' of the child used in civil cases, children moved from being a universal group to becoming individuals.

> If the law should impose upon the process of growing up fixed limits where nature knows only a continuous process, the price would be artificially and a lack of realism in an area where the law must be sensitive to human development and social change…a minor's capacity to make his or her own decision depends upon the minor having sufficient understanding and intelligence to make the decision and is not to be determined by reference to any fixed age limit. (Gillick v West Norfolk HA, 1986 1 FLR 250)

From these starting points challenges increased to those views of the 'universal child'. These are reflected in many different studies of social life as the importance of the individual became (and continues to become) of increasing focus.

In short, if we are prepared to recognise children as individuals then we start to see children in terms of their feelings and emotions, their sense of right and wrong, their experiences, beliefs, sense of self and more. It means that when a child speaks, they don't represent the identical views of all other children; rather, they represent a view that is unique and personal to them.

By recognising the individual we are also able to understand the value attached to their voice.

B. Future Child to Active Child

As we have seen, a dominant 'noise' or way of thinking is that children should be seen in terms of what they will become. This has meant that we have not been good at engaging with children based on who they are now. Children are 'becomings', but they are also 'beings' – contributing to the here and now. Indeed, aren't all of us both beings and becomings?

The idea that we are all beings and becomings creates the image of a journey that each and every one of us is on. In the past, the category of citizen was defined by the higher level of competence that certain groups in society were seen to have. Over time increasing numbers were recognised as citizens, which was reflected in their access to certain rights; for example, the ability to vote or to access certain welfare rights and benefits. However, due to their perceived lack of competence, children remained outside of this definition of citizen.

Here, we need to be part of encouraging a shift in the notion of citizenship itself. Research is highlighting how our understandings of what it means to be a citizen increasingly reflects a role that we as individuals might play in shaping 'what might be termed' a 'common good'. Citizenship is therefore defined in relation to efforts to be inclusive, as demonstrated through the widest level of social engagement. This, of course, begs the question – what does this mean for children? For if we accept that children are both beings and becomings then they have a role to play now as citizens (Bacon and Frankel 2014).

A common good cannot be defined by those with particular qualifications or status, rather it must be the product of all of us. This theme to some extent shapes Unicef's Child Friendly Cities project. Children have a contribution to make; if we want a common good that is truly *common* then we need to increase those opportunities to activate the voice of the child.

C. Protected Child to Participating Child

For the protected child to become the participating child adults need to value and not feel threatened by children having a voice.

The protected child is easy to maintain control of, but what about the participating child? An example of adult fears over inviting children's participation can be seen in relation to the voting age.

In 2015 the UK government gave children aged 16 and 17 the vote as part of the referendum on whether Scotland should leave the United Kingdom. Children were seen as having a clear stake in the argument as it was their futures they were deciding. However, when it came some months later to the vote for the UK to leave the EU the same children were told that they were no longer seen as capable of providing a competent and considered opinion. Why was this? Whatever the answer, it makes a statement about adult ambitions to act in the best interest of the child ahead of a child's right to participate.

The extent to which adults are willing to cede power to children is a thorny issue. Adults remain cautious about giving children a voice in areas where this may carry the weight to bring about change. What this results in is a culture of tokenism. However, the contribution that children's voices can and do make must not be underestimated.

CASE STUDIES

The *divorce system* has long held the belief that children should be protected rather than given the chance to participate. In Canada and around the world, however, increasingly systems are recognising the need for children to have a voice. Through having a voice children feel that they are able to make some contribution. Notably, fears that increasing the prominence of children's voices would mean adults losing some control have not been realised. In fact, it has not necessarily been a desire to be able to make the 'choice' that children have been encouraged by, but merely the chance to have a voice.

Schools are environments where adults remain nervous about reducing the clear and defined pathways of authority. However, what research is showing is that children's feelings towards adult practices of classroom management where they are not consulted have a negative impact on children's learning. This is in contrast to models in which, through a focus on children's rights, the power structure is altered and children's voices are valued, as adults and children work their way together towards an effective solution (Urinboyev *et al.* 2016).

Children's best interests cannot be assumed and a desire merely to protect the child will ultimately never establish the best interests of a community as a whole. Allowing children to have a voice can lead to more effective outcomes for all.

A culture of advocacy will inform a true ambition for a common good.

Reflection

1. Think back to the 'noise' you identified in Step 1. Consider whether you have missed anything? Is there some 'noise' that highlights the more active image of the child?

2. Often this noise is much softer, therefore we might need to search harder for it. Where might we search? How can we increase the volume?

ACTION 7: IMAGINE THE DIFFERENCE

As suggested above, the way we think about children profoundly impacts on how we engage with children.

- Do we view children in terms of their universality or their individuality?

- Are children to be assessed in terms of what they lack or in terms of what they offer?

- Should adults be seen as the sole arbiters of a child's 'best interests'?

How we answer these questions will directly shape our approach to advocacy, both in terms of what we see as its purpose and in relation to how we view children's involvement.

We are surrounded by so much 'noise' about the child, which impacts our thinking and shapes our views. That noise and related assumptions might come in the form of what we hear on the news, what we read in a book; it might be based on experiences or professional training. It might be based on our interpretation of laws or customs or conversations in our communities and on the way things have been done in the past. All this gets jumbled around in our minds, weighted in different ways to produce an 'image' of the child.

This image shapes practices which then impact on children's experiences.

In closing this first 'step', we need to be clear what our personal ethos is for engaging with children. If we wish to see children as partners in society then we need to challenge our image of the child, re-imagining a culture in which the image of the child that dominates is one that reflects children as individuals, as active and as participants. Such images will change practices and alter children's experiences. In short, our thinking on engaging with children has the power to bring about social revolution!

Reflection

Re-imagine the previous actions. What changes do you need to make? What difference would it result in?

BE SPATIALLY AWARE

Part 1: Creating a climate for change	Step 1 – Revitalise your thinking!	
	Step 2 – Be spatially aware	8. Have review criteria: your motivation, your image
		9. Plan your review: what to look at
		10. Start a conversation
Section objectives		• To develop an understanding of assessment measures that can bring rhetoric in line with reality. • To be able to identify areas of an organisation that can provide a focus for assessment. • To raise awareness of methods to promote conversations creating space for children's voices to be heard.

Often a school principal will be very happy to tell you about 'their' school. However, in one conversation the principal told me, 'Well, of course I never say "my" school because it isn't mine, it's theirs [the children's].' This comment establishes the challenge for this chapter. In the spaces where we engage with children it is very easy for adults to take control. However, here the ambition is about reflecting on how the nature of that space offers a real opportunity for a coming together, to create a shared space and a community that reflects a common purpose in which children's voices are heard.

In many ways, therefore, this chapter is as much about detoxing those spaces that we share with children as the last chapter was about detoxing ourselves.

It is really important that we recognise that the spaces and settings we talk about in this chapter include both the formal spaces we share with children (such as schools, a courtroom, a doctor's consulting room and so on) and informal spaces (which include home, the local playground). The steps within this chapter are probably easier to implement in relation to those formal spaces but that does not mean they will not also work in informal spaces too (we just might need to be a little more creative).

A culture of advocacy is of course defined by our ambition to:

- establish the child's voice: children's voices are acknowledged and valued

- amplify the child's voice: opportunities are created that allow children's voices to be heard, giving others the chance to respond or engage.

The steps in this chapter are intended to help us to see how a culture of advocacy can evolve within those spaces. As with the previous chapter, this will involve us questioning and challenging the way we think about children and reflecting on this as we seek to refresh our views and set our engagement with children up to be as effective as possible.

SETTING THE TONE – RHETORIC VS REALITY

Within the spaces where we interact with children it is possible to identify particular 'approaches' to the child. These approaches will be shaped by the individuals that form part of these spaces. However, unlike the previous chapter, where we were focusing on an individually held view, here we recognise a group of individuals and images of the child coming together; a variety of views which are focused through, amongst other things, the purpose of that space, by internal policies or practices and, to varying extents, external laws.

The result is that within that space a 'culture' or 'approach' to the child comes to take shape.

As part of this, a 'tone' is set for how children are to be engaged with.

CASE STUDY

Gustoso is a local Italian restaurant. It states that it is 'child friendly'.

The management decide it is time to change the menu. However, even in this 'child friendly' restaurant, they decide to do this without any consultation.

The first sign that they had made a mistake was when pizza after pizza was returned to the kitchen. The problem was that children were not keen on the new parsley topping.

The second problem came when children tried to order something other than the pepperoni and parsley pizza that was the only pizza on the children's menu. The new computer system that the management had implemented would not let the servers alter a child's pizza – they could not change or add to this one topping. This was the complete opposite to an adult ordering a pizza, in which case the computer offered prompts to the server to find out if any additional toppings were required.

The result was that children were stuck with pepperoni and parsley pizzas!

Gustoso has a particular approach towards the child. Indeed, like many other organisations Gustoso's approach declares that they are child friendly. However, behind the rhetoric is a reality that is clearly different. Here, adults made choices that did not reflect on how children might come to experience the decisions that were being made on their behalf.

Importantly, if Gustoso had been more aware of their approach towards the child, if they had been able to link rhetoric and reality, then this would have had positive consequences for their customer satisfaction and also their commercial success. The case here is that a culture of advocacy is not simply about an idealistic desire to give children a voice, it also makes sense. Even in the hard-nosed world of business, a culture of advocacy can further a profit margin. Similarly, in the equally challenging environment of non-profit organisations, engaging with children's voices can be reflected in the benefits that such organisations seek to offer and the power of the message they are able to communicate.

CASE STUDY

The UK has been caught up in a new era of enlightenment created by the harrowing uncovering of years of systemic child abuse (Casey 2015). What case after case is showing is that an 'image' of the child has existed that restricted or rejected the value of children's voices. Here, the rhetoric of care within organisations was not matched by the reality of their practice.

One startling example is the Rotherham abuse case, which shows how the image of the child that had been constructed by professionals (in the police and social care services) restricted the support that these children were able to access. In fact, rather than finding help, the children simply received condemnation and judgement.

Victims found themselves placed outside of a duty of care because they were seen as different to other children. Here these girls, who were regularly being raped and abused by older men, were seen in terms of the 'life style choices' they had made. Their voices were de-valued, to the point where their cries were ignored.

One victim said that she was accused of lying when she spoke out about the abuse:

They didn't believe me...they told me I was trouble... nobody listened, I had police officers take me back to these men. (BBC 2015).

Another victim reported suffering many attacks over five years. She said, 'they [the gang] felt they were fearless and untouchable...the police said I was asking for it...I had no voice to speak. No-one listened' (BBC 2015).

The major lesson from these cases was that no one was questioning or challenging the approach to the child that had been adopted. The rest of this chapter is therefore dedicated to finding ways in which the spaces we share with children can be interrogated and in which the 'tone' that is set acknowledges in both rhetoric and reality the importance and value of children's voices.

DEVELOPING YOUR SPATIAL AWARENESS

We have thought about getting our personal ethos towards children right. However, it is just as important that we consider this in relation to those spaces or settings where we engage with children.

Below, therefore, are some steps that make visible the approach to children in a setting, and through which we can then seek to tackle that rhetoric/reality gap. Indeed, even if the spaces you share with children are already doing all those things that create an environment for a culture of advocacy to flourish, it is important to find a way to continue to reflect on this to ensure that it is maintained and kept healthy.

Below is a framework that we are going to explore.

Action 8: It is important to define the criteria that we will use as part of any assessment. Here, these will be:

- motivation

- image of the child.

Action 9: Once we know our review criteria – the next question is, what should we examine? We will consider:

- what you are trying to say
- what you are trying to do
- how children are represented.

Action 10: To have impact, the aim is that our review will then 'start a conversation'.

ACTION 8: HAVE REVIEW CRITERIA

Our approaches towards children might be driven by a very real ambition to do the best for the child. However, wouldn't it be helpful if in pursuing this ambition we could be made aware of the dangers that come from misplaced assumptions? The 'actions' in this chapter are there to identify areas where rhetoric and reality do not match, offering settings the chance to re-focus and ensure that children's voices are more effectively engaged with. This will be considered through looking at:

- motivation
- the image of the child.

Motivation

Consider, what is it that drives the approach to the child in this setting? The following four criteria provide a simple way to explore or consider motivation.

	Definition
Protect	Ensuring that the child is safe (and that, through policies towards the child, society more widely is safe).
	This term 'protect' does seem to have a broad interpretation. Approaches within traditional advocacy have highlighted how a protectionist approach towards the child can also be used to argue for measures that control and constrain the child. It justifies this approach towards the child by suggesting that intrusive steps to manage the child are justified protection – protecting them from themselves, whilst protecting them from the harm they might do to others! This can be seen in justifications for policies such as the use of the criminal law, which protects the child (bringing them into the system) and protects us.
Provide	Ensuring that the child, and those connected with them, have what's needed for a given standard of life.
	Provision, like protection, must be examined by recognising the wider needs that adults are seeking to pursue for the child. For example, provision might be fuelled by a future ambition to ensure that children can be an effective future workforce and thus improve the country's economic growth. Provision can, therefore, be reflected in political idealism as part of a search for answers that are thought to best address the needs of the child and society.
Participate	Ensuring that children have actual opportunities to engage and get involved in meaningful and valued ways.
	Participation is always easy to talk about, but not so stridently put into practice. So although organisations may claim participation as a motivation, the important aspect in the assessment process is a consideration of the actual and meaningful ways in which it is put into practice.
Profit	Ensuring that children are used for the benefit of adult goals (whether financial or otherwise).
	Children's exploitation at the hands of adults is real. For too many adults their motivation for engaging with children is driven by a desire to gain some benefit, without consideration of the cost to the child. This might take the form of children working in a factory, through to the use of a particular image of the child as helpless, innocent or poor to lend weight to a campaign or argument.

The value of participation

You may recognise the connection of these terms to the earlier discussion on children's rights. Children's rights, mentioned in the last chapter, offer a useful measure to support the way in which we might come to approach advocacy.

The problem is that children's rights are not perfect. Indeed, the model for children's rights that was put in place in 1989 and which has since become the most signed international convention, the United Nations Convention on the Rights of the Child (UNCRC), developed out of a particular context. That context was seen by many as excessively Western and notably adult dominated. The result is that the convention is arguably a document defined by adults, for the use of adults. The adult-centric application of this document is reinforced by the limited number of children that actually know about it.

Some figures suggest that 70 per cent of children don't know of the UNCRC (James and James 2004). On many occasions, we have not been surprised to find that – both with groups of younger children and with students at university – no one has heard about it. If you want to find out the level of knowledge, ask some children and see – we would be interested to know what you find.

As a result the UNCRC itself can be subject to an analysis around motivation. How does the rhetoric match the reality? Growing out of a wider community view that was in place in the 1920s following World War I, when a drive to create an international document began, the child was seen in terms of whether they were safe and whether their needs were effectively provided for, as the importance of moving children away from systems motivated by 'profit' grew. As such 'protection' and 'provision' became a driving focus. Within this, it was seen that if 'protection' and 'provision' were effectively administered then this paved the way for children's 'participation'. Arguably, that sense of 'participation' was seen in terms of children's future value as contributors to the workforce, rather than their value whilst children.

As such it creates the following:

Protection + Provision = Participation

Although this focus on protection and provision can be easily noted within the rights agenda, the key question is whether protection and provision are best served by having participation as an 'added extra'. The contention here is that this model needs to look like this (see Frankel, McNamee and Pomfret 2015):

Participation = Protection & Provision

Through a focus on children's participation, establishing their voices and then amplifying them, we are in a stronger position to both identify what children need and how best they should be protected. As we consider the nature of effective spaces for advocacy, therefore, *motivation* is key. Does the space that has been created seek to focus on assumed understandings around the protection and provision of children by adults, or does it seek to engage with need and safety through children's participation, building a broader understanding of the issues?

Notably, this does not mean that adults should be any less ambitions about protecting and providing for children, rather it demands that we seek to be better informed, through inviting children's participation in responding to the issues *they* face.

Our engagement with motivation can be further refined by adding this to a consideration of the image of the child which we started in the previous chapter.

The image of the child

Our motivation will be defined by the image of the child that we hold.

In the last chapter we touched on the complex way in which images of the child come to be constructed. The consequence of this is that there are a multitude of images; however, as part of evaluating and assessing an approach, it can sometimes be helpful to have some defined categories to direct our thinking.

The following criteria offer a simple tool. You can always add to this by drawing from the images considered in the last chapter (see Resource Sheet 2).

List of images	Description	Amount reflected in setting	Conclusion (assessment of image in that setting)
Object	Views the child as simply a specimen to be observed		
Subject	Acknowledges the particular nature of the child and the importance of engaging with it – although this remains adult-directed		
Social agent	Recognises children's potential as competent and active participants (but without creating opportunities for this to be put into practice)		
Co-participant	Not only acknowledges children as social agents above, but also actively creates opportunities for their participation including change-making activities with adults		

The 'image' will define the type of advocacy approach that adults, in the context of a setting, will deliver. If we see children as subjects or objects, our approach to advocacy will be driven by the need for us, as adults, to act on their behalf. If, however, we see children as agents, then we recognise that our role becomes one of facilitator for the child, as we seek to allow them to share their voice as value is given to their individual contribution. Step 5 will introduce the idea of the 'active coach', which explores further the role of adults, particularly in the context of adults and children as co-participants.

CASE STUDY

Canada, as its response to embedding the UNCRC, directed each province to set up a Child Advocacy Office. What has been interesting about this process is the variety of ways in which these offices have approached advocacy with children. Indeed, a review of all these offices offers a very clear example of the way in which the image of the child comes to impact on the practices that develop. The two most contrasting positions are reflected below. They offer an illustration of the range of approaches that can exist within the same system. Here the use of the assessment criteria offers a means to highlight the differences. Although both offices display rhetoric that highlights their ambitions for the child, the reality of their practice is very different.

Child Advocacy Office	Motivation	Image	Approach to advocacy
Quebec: Commission des Droits de la Personne et des Droits de la Jeunesse[1]	Protect	Object	The image is defined by children's place as a legal object. As such, advocacy is approached as a task that adults complete on behalf of the child. Action is taken in response to adult referrals, although children are able to make a phone call. Beyond this call, children's participation is not sought, as this approach to advocacy relies on adult commitments to protection and provision in response to an assumed image of the child.
Ontario: The Office of the Provincial Advocate for Children and Youth[2]	Participate	Co-participant	Here the emphasis is on listening to and learning from children, as adults seek to facilitate children's voices, placing them at the centre of the advocacy process. As part of an interesting definition of advocacy which is shared on their website they declare: The primary goal of child advocacy is to elevate the voice of youth. This means more than empowering youth to speak out on their own behalf. It means more than faithfully replaying their words. The standard to aspire to is articulated in an African proverb: 'Don't speak about us, without us.' It means speaking together with youth about youth. This has resulted in children being involved in a range of ways: from highlighting areas for investigation, the sharing and collecting of evidence, through to offering recommendations to policy makers. Project examples – Youth Leaving Care, Feather's of Hope and I Have Something to Say – see the website for more. Youth Committees – Children involved in these committees meet on a regular basis to discuss their projects and the next steps. Youth involved in these committees are referred to as Youth Amplifiers and Youth Advisors.

[1] www.cdpdj.qc.ca/en [2] www.provincialadvocate.on.ca

ACTION 9: PLANNING A REVIEW

Your review can reflect on motivation and the image of the child in relation to the following:

- What are you trying to say?

- What are you trying to do?

- How are children represented?

What are you trying to say?

Spaces are infused with words. The visibility of a narrative around children is far more apparent in formal spaces – but that does not mean it is not also present in the informal spaces (from the notices that might be up around a playground, to the house rules we might set and then attach to the fridge).

These words will say something about us and more importantly about how we view children and adults within a given space. These words create a 'tone' towards the child – one that offers a collective motivation and image, which in formal contexts might come to be displayed in strategic policies, in development plans, annual reviews, on websites and in newsletters, and the list could go on. It is not just in written documents that that this tone can be identified but also in the way in which people talk and discuss children in the context of your organisation or setting.

What are you trying to do?

Another area for assessment is the nature of the activities or practices that form within an organisation or setting.

By considering the nature of the actions, we can get a sense of the motivation that sits behind them. This, too, might then feed into the image of the child that we construe in relation to that setting.

Professional engagement with children is one area in which the rhetoric/reality gap is very real. It is no good talking the talk, if one is not also able to walk the walk. Professionals may be very good at presenting a co-participatory view of the child – thus demonstrating 'participation' as their motivation; however, the reality is not always so clear cut.

CASE STUDY

This example is a little dated, but the themes it raises remain highly relevant. In this investigation researchers focused on the process of teachers creating a classroom code with their children. A key focus was teachers' attitudes towards the children. Although these teachers invited the children's input, the pervading image of the child was one that reflected those notions of universality, incompetence and the need to maintain control. Having observed staff practices the researchers findings included the following results: that 'the teacher knows best', that teachers perceive children as being unable to participate in creating the constitution, that they are not really interested or have the moral capacity (which teachers do have) and that if the children were given responsibility 'chaos might result' (Sarason 1971).

When the teachers in this study were shown the results they were very surprised. They had not recognised the extent to which the dominant image of the child that was held in school had so significantly influenced their practices within the classroom.

How are children represented?

The third way we are able to assess and evaluate the space a community creates for effective advocacy is by considering how the child is presented and what opportunities or platforms there are for their voices to be heard.

Key to this is the visibility of the voice of the child within the organisation. This might come through:

- participative activities – children on strategic bodies, children as researchers

- overt public presence – the visibility of children's voices as a basis for defining strategy

- strategic planning – the extent to which operating procedures within an organisation demand ongoing consideration of children's voices as part of shaping day-to-day activities.

The important thing is that children's voices are not merely tokenistic.

CASE STUDY

This case study draws on a student's experience of school council (Lewars 2010). Lewars' article suggested that schools were very happy to allow a school council to meet just so long as the teachers defined the topics that the school council was able to engage with. As a result, the school council found itself dealing with the less controversial issues ('most commonly toilets, school dinners and student parties') (Lewars 2010, p.234). The issues about which pupils were keen to have a say, however, included 'lessons; homework; appointment or induction of staff; discipline/punishment; school rules; code of behaviour' (Lewars 2010, p.234). Unfortunately these topics were regarded by adults as 'off limits'. School councils thus become tokenistic, as schools fulfilled a requirement, rather than making the most of an opportunity to engage with children's voices:

> it is not difficult to imagine the relief of a teacher who is
> seriously against student involvement in decision making,
> as they can simply set up a 'puppet' school council to
> decide on the colour of the uniform, or other trivialities.
> (Lewars 2010, p.271)

The danger is that how we come to represent children's voices
can be seen as a tick box exercise, rather than really opening up
opportunities for their active participation. This is particularly
relevant to children who are seen not only through the lens
of being a child but also through an additional lens such as
having a disability or being a member of a migrant community.
In such cases, we need to question more deeply whether the
opportunities created are meaningful, as we assess this in light
of whether the individual knows and understands that their
voice is valued.

ACTION 10: STARTING A CONVERSATION

An assessment can be carried out into what is written and also
what is spoken. Exploring both allows you to investigate the
strength of the connection between rhetoric and reality.

What is written?

The first place to start is the 'shop window'. What is the public
message that an organisation sends? A website can offer a useful
indication. Other public messages might be shared through
social media, the press, promotional materials, publications or
presentations.

   If one were looking at a website one might investigate:

- Mission or Vision Statement

- An organisational aim – some blurb that defines what
   you are about

- A description of your activities or purpose

- Your annual review of newsletters.

Reviewing these will offer a sense of the image/motivation. You can record your findings in Resource Sheet 3.

Element of Focus	Assessment of Motivation	Assessment of Image	Recommendations
	What are you trying to say? What are you trying to do? How are children's voices represented?		
Website			
Annual review			
Project description			
Newsletter			

Reflection

You might like to try out using this table. Try reflecting on the website for the Children's Commissioner in Wales – which has much to recommend it – www.childcomwales.org.uk.

Note: Do not forget those informal spaces too!

What is spoken?

Organising a focus group

The public face of an organisation offers one important insight. But what about the day to day? A home, for example, is a space in which the value of a well-maintained website might not be very obvious. To get a more detailed view it is, therefore, important to talk to people. By engaging with those within an organisation, one is able to review that rhetoric/reality gap and to consider further the motivation and image of the child as you compare what is written and what is spoken.

Within an organisation it would be worth asking these same questions to:

- senior managers

- workers

- children.

Try to get a focus group (a discussion with a small group of people – around 4) made up of:

- one group of senior managers

- two groups of workers

- four groups of children.

By contrasting the results of the questions below you will be in a position to then assess the image and motivation of the organisation.

Note: you can also try this activity for an informal setting too, for example, as part of a parenting forum or group.

Some simple questions

Here are some questions which will inform your analysis. Ask the questions and then listen to the discussion and make notes (see the table on the next page).

- How do you see children?

- How do you see adults?

- Where do you hear children's voices? (How do the groups you are talking with define children's voices, what examples can they give of children's voices in action?)

Come up with a couple of your own questions which you think will allow you to assess your organisation or setting.

Analysis

Use the table (on the following page) to help you to gather your thoughts and begin your analysis. (See Resource Sheet 4.)

Senior manager: You would expect a strong and clear assessment of how they and the organisation see the child and their voice. If their organisation is motivated by participation, a senior manager should be able to clearly share that, explaining what that means in terms of their understanding of the child but also the role of adults, as they seek to support children's engagement.

Workers: Does the view of the workers mirror that of the senior manager? Do both groups share the same image of the child? The discussion around these questions should allow elements of this to emerge. You will also want to reflect on whether the practical realities of the tasks that 'workers' run or deliver with children impact on the image that they hold.

Element of focus	Notes of conversation	Assessment of motivation	Assessment of image	Recommendations
		Language	Activities to establish voice of child	
			Representation of voice	
How do you see children?	**Tip:** You will need to keep a record of the conversations so you can compare your findings and develop your analysis.			
	You can do this through asking your participants to record their ideas on a sheet of paper as they go. For example, ask them to write down key words on how they see children.			
How do you see adults?	Use a separate sheet of paper for each new question and then repeat with each group.			
Where do you hear children's voices?	You can make notes alongside their key words as they speak. This will give you a simple record of the conversation.			
Your own questions	For a more detailed record you may wish to record what is said and then turn this into a short transcript.			

Children: This contrast can be really interesting and very powerful. Adults might see themselves as very caring and encouraging, children however might see the adults as 'shouty' and 'grumpy'. These differences would indicate that rhetoric/reality gap and would thus play a major part in shaping the image of the child that you assess that organisation actually has.

Look out for:

- contrasting views between adults and children

- commonalities, or not, between words that describe the organisation or their activities

- talk and understanding around voice (from different perspectives).

Tip: if you are using the sheets of paper to record key words as suggested on the previous page, then a useful analysis can be carried out simply by comparing the answers of the different groups to the same questions.

Keep on researching

The questions above should have given you enough information to begin your assessment. However, there might be more you want to know. To investigate further, you could continue your conversation through:

- a questionnaire

- observations

- the anonymous sharing of ideas (a letterbox where people – children and adults – can post their thoughts).

For more on 'research' see Step 3 and Action Research in Step 5.

CONCLUSION

By now you should be able to assess motivation and the image of the child within a setting and, as a result of this, promote a conversation about the nature of that setting and how it might move towards being an effective space for children to be heard.

Steps 3, 4 and 5 will help to define those next steps as you journey towards your own culture of advocacy.

CASE STUDIES

The final part of this chapter offers some case studies. These are written by some of my old students, Lindsay Izsac and Nadine Ivancovik, who found that whilst taking a course in Childhood Studies their eyes were opened to a range of different social settings. They have, therefore, offered some reflections on these settings, showing how a heightened sense of awareness has led them to question and challenge traditional ways of engaging with children and how valuing a culture of advocacy can make a real difference.

Restaurants – a space for children's participation

My (Nadine's) experience of working in restaurants is that parents often make choices for children.

I remember one night when two families came into the restaurant. One child, after waiting for his turn, ordered correctly, asking for fish and also ordering a side of cucumber, showing good knowledge of how the menu worked. However, as soon as he had ordered his dad said 'no'. He ordered him a hot dog instead without any effort to explain why. It just seemed like an opportunity for a parent to assert their power, to show they were in control.

A restaurant, however, has the potential to be an effective environment within which opportunities can be created for children to practice using their voice.

Children have the capacity to state their opinions on where to eat and what to eat. When children are viewed as an equal customer, the dining out experience changes. Simply by staff getting down to children's level, by asking clear questions and taking their ideas seriously, a restaurant can become a space that children really feel a part of. Restaurants are a perfect example of everyday situations where children can be given greater opportunities to use their voice, which, if encouraged, can have a whole load of positive results.

Valuing children's opinions on spaces like restaurants could also change the way in which department stores and many other businesses operate.

Engaging community groups – the 60s scoop

The 60s scoop is a term used to refer to a time in Canada from the 1960s to the 1980s when the removal of aboriginal children from their homes was accelerated. Social workers believed that practices within the home meant that these children were facing neglect and abuse and therefore they needed to be protected. By the 1970s, one in three aboriginal children was placed into the Child Welfare System.

The experiences of the children during this time are full of tragedy. Their voices were simply not heard.

Throughout, the children were seen as objects. What would have happened if those key workers had had a different image of these children, in which they wanted to 'co-participate' and to work alongside aboriginal families? Personally, I (Lindsay) believe that this would have greatly altered the history that we know today. Unfortunately, the objective view of children and the dominance of adults advocating on behalf of instead of with children is not an isolated event and continues today within these communities. This leaves me to wonder, have we truly learnt from the past, or are we merely letting history continue to be rewritten?

An eye opening account of these policies is portrayed in Alanis Obomsawin's short film, *Richard Cardinal: Cry from the diary of a Métis Child*.[1]

Children's role in and around the legal process – divorce

Currently, children's voices are severely limited within the realm of divorce and other family related matters. The United Nations Convention of the Right of the Child (UNCRC) outlines the rights and responsibilities that adults have towards young people. Although all the articles should collectively promote children's participation it can be easier to track engagement with rights such as Article 3 than Articles 12 or 13. Article 3 states that 'In all actions concern children, whether undertaken by public or private social welfare institutions, courts of law, administrative authorities or legislative bodies, the best interests of the child shall be a primary consideration'. The problem is that the best interests is often interpreted from an adult perspective. Even though adults are encouraged by Article 12 to think about children's participation, how that is done remains subjective as adults often maintain control.

This is particularly pronounced in the context of the legal system, where it is clear that children have been marginalized within divorce and familial breakup due to being viewed as vulnerable and in need of protection by adults. As a result of this standpoint protection and provision rights are seen as fundamental and thus hold priority over participation rights. This means that

1   www.nfb.ca/film/richard_cardinal

participation rights, although noted as important within legislation fall through the cracks and commonly remain neglected throughout the process. Even though these actions reflect a desire to act for the children's well-being, this comes at the cost of a lack of engagement with opportunities through which children can participate.

Children want to feel important and that they are a part of such a major family event. The result of a court case will impact them too, it is therefore important that parents and other adults fully engage with their role within the process. The danger is that the Best Interests of the Child comes to override any form of children's participation unless we find a way to break the cycle.

A local law project in London Ontario is an example of an organization that strives to assist families through divorce, custody and access disputes. Some of the programs they use to assist families experiencing divorce include 'custody and access assessment', 'mediation', and 'parenting coordination'. The common thread between all of these programs is the use of a neutral third party who intends to act as a mediator to the parents and adults involved. However, our assessment is that this approach is too easily shaped by the Best Interests Doctrine such that the voice of the child is never effectively heard.

So how can children be included in divorce and custody disputes within families and what are their views regarding the spaces that are or are not available to them? The first step is recognizing children as equal members of the family with shared and unique experiences within the divorce experience. Listening to children's perspective is not only beneficial to the parents and children separately but rather to the family as a whole. It is important to note that children do not ask for decision making power within conflicts, they just wish to be recognized as individuals who have something valuable to offer to the discussion. Studies have concluded that children who have been included in discussions regarding custody have experienced higher levels of satisfaction, feeling more relaxed and better able to cope with the change in family structure. Adults have an important role in ensuring that this is achieved, both adult professionals and parents should advocate alongside children to ensure that they are granted these opportunities. Children can participate by expressing their thoughts to parents, attending an interview with a judge in chamber, appointing a children's lawyer or speaking with a family mediator.

We suggest that this needs to be done in a safe, open and meaningful environment where children are encouraged to speak the truth without experiencing any negative repercussions. Children 's participation does not have to be a complex or frustrating process with many people involved. Rather including children in these matters can be as simple as being honest with them, answering their questions and listening to their thoughts. Through this a participatory space for children is not only being achieved within custody disputes but can also be relevant in all aspects of family life. Ultimately this would better achieve the best interest of the child, as they understand that the adults around them truly care about what they feel and think, as the child's voice helps to shape our understanding of 'their best interests'.

Advertising campaigns

Adverts for children are big business. Companies have recognised that if they can harness 'pester' power then this can lead to greater sales. Many of us are concerned about the popularity of these commercials and the negative impact that they may have on children. Countries are looking for ways to 'protect' their children from the force of the advert as seen in the 'Campaign for a Commercial Free Childhood'[2] already supported by countries like Norway and Sweden. Within this campaign there are ten key foci. What is interesting about the campaign is that we found no evidence of children being spoken to about what advertisements are, how to recognise and understand them properly and, finally, how to make smart purchases.

An alternative approach might be to use education to increase children's media literacy, raising their awareness of what is a want and a need, the value of money (saving and spending), and the place and purposes of commercial incitements. Engaging with children and giving them a voice to recognise and respond to commercials means that a commercial offers a learning moment, rather than something to be feared and avoided.[3]

2   www.commercialfreechildhood.org/resource/ten-things-you-can-do-reclaim-childhood-corporate-marketers
3   See Media Smart – www.mediasmart.uk.com.

PART 2

TURNING RHETORIC INTO REALITY

In Part 1 we questioned and interrogated both ourselves and the spaces in which we engage with children. Part 2 is about how those spaces come to change, or indeed how you maintain a change that has already happened, one that reflects and is focused on pursuing a culture of advocacy.

The following three steps therefore focus on the extent to which a culture of advocacy comes to be embedded in an organisation. The value of these ideas is only fully effective when it spreads to every part of our engagement with children in these different spaces where we interact with them. These ideas do not represent a programme that can be delivered on a Tuesday afternoon or a Friday morning in a one-hour slot; rather they are about creating a way of thinking and doing that needs to inform all aspects of our engagement with children all of the time.

To help us consider how a culture of advocacy comes to be embedded we will focus on our next three steps:

- Step 3 – Speak the right language

- Step 4 – Create opportunities

- Step 5 – Lead the change.

These themes do interlink and all feed into creating that space within which a culture of advocacy can thrive. At the centre of all of this is the importance of creating opportunities to:

- establish children's voices
- offer platforms that allow those voices to be heard and acted on.

SPEAK THE RIGHT LANGUAGE

Part 1: Creating a climate for change	Step 1 – Revitalise your thinking!	
	Step 2 – Be spatially aware	
Part 2: Turning rhetoric into reality	Step 3 – Speak the right language	11. Set characteristics
		12. Develop a technical vocabulary: • participation • research • connecting to emotions.
Section objectives		Identify attributes or characteristics that will provide a focus for attention to promote the voice of the individual Create a language to allow for effective : • participation, • research, • effective communication.

The first element that is required in order to ensure a culture of advocacy will work in practice is a shared language.

A lack of clarity can be an essential ingredient in entertainment (whether in a TV soap or in a play), where a misunderstanding over language can drive a whole storyline, either for the purposes of comedy or tragedy. Here, however, clarity about language is vital to help shape an environment in which a culture of advocacy can be made both accessible and meaningful.

Step 3 invites you to think about the nature of language in developing a culture of advocacy. This will include considering our vocabulary and the need for this vocabulary to be shared within a setting.

Note: Your aim should not be to clone a language used by others but rather to develop a language that makes sense for you. This step offers some 'tools' that you can use to help shape that language.

ACTION 11: SET CHARACTERISTICS

This action helps create a shortcut to a positive working image of the child, through defining a set of characteristics, which will frame practice and shape children's experiences.

At the heart of a culture of advocacy is an ambition to create a learning opportunity for children that will further their ability to navigate the complex social world they are part of. Our ability to know what type of opportunities we need to create will be directed by what it is that we want children to get out of our interactions with them. To know this we need to make visible those attributes we would like to give children an experience of.

An important aspect of our work in schools is to be clear about the nature and types of learning opportunities that school should be about creating. We do this through inviting schools, in consultation with children and adults, to set out a list of characteristics or attributes that the children are going to be able to engage with during their time in school and which, significantly, create a basis on which to build discussion, focus practices and create opportunities.

These will be specific to that learning community. Their value lies in making visible the processes that connect those personal and social skills with one's effectiveness as a learner, as effort is put into encouraging a positive attitude, effective communication, the ability to take a risk and so on. If we are to encourage a culture of advocacy it is a useful activity for us to have some sense of what learning opportunities children will get the chance to experience.

In the context of this book, the focus is around children's voices and may include characteristics such as:

- valuing my voice and that of others

- being confident in expressing my voice

- understanding different means of communication

- growing as a leader.

These, of course, can be added to. The depth here is going to depend on the nature of the setting and the type of interaction. We simply want to create something that others can engage with too. Short and concise is a very good starting place (which can, if needed, be added to in time). For more ideas, see Frankel and Fowler (2016).

Note: Your characteristics or attributes will be shaped by the conversations you started in Step 2. As these develop invite children and adults to help frame what these characteristics are.

Before undertaking the activity, have a look at the following case studies.

CASE STUDIES

School

Hapley School was full of ambition and ideas. The staff were motivated and so were the children. But what was it that they were motivated to achieve? The staff knew the school had a motto, the children did too, but no one knew what it actually meant. The children knew that they had a role, but neither adult nor child could consistently tell you what that was. What the school needed was a language through which they could define that role and that purpose of the child within school.

Why was this important?

- It allowed the school to reflect on their image of the child and create a common and shared view.

- It provided a focus for school practices and the basis for shaping opportunities.

- It allowed the school to see what they were doing well.

- It allowed the school to evaluate and measure where the gaps in provision were.

- It provided a language through which everyone (children and adults) could discuss and engage with 'learning'.

The act of us defining 'characteristics'or goals within our setting provides a focus for attention (idea development, review and evaluation).

Criminal justice

A 2014 report by a UK Parliamentary Group (APPGC 2014) showed how trust was a significant issue in terms of the relationship that the police had with children. One area that might have been worth including within the recommendations is a greater consideration of what opportunities the police were trying to create for children.

A project by a group of my students in Canada focused on the experience of children at the police station. Their conclusion was that children's ability to be part of a process of advocacy was removed because there were no 'child friendly' materials to explain what their rights were. As such, children were merely objects in a set of practices that were happening around them. If we are to encourage children to take responsibility, then surely an important step is to establish some characteristics that invite the police to see children in a more 'active' way. Creating a standard for engagement could move interactions away from being a negative experience to something far more constructive.

Is this an impractical dream? No. The work that is being done around restorative justice shows the very positive effect that a focus on certain characteristics such as responsibility, empathy and forgiveness is having on the way children come to reflect on their behaviour.

Restorative justice

This case study is from Sarah Kuchyt (one of my former students who was undertaking a placement at a restorative justice programme in Ontario, Canada).

What stood out for me, experiencing a restorative justice programme for the first time, was just how much of an opportunity it gave young people who had got into trouble the chance to really think about the issues. It gave them a chance to think about what they had done and why, and how they felt about it now. However, the programme never left them feeling out of control. They were part of it. In fact I think that their active involvement throughout the process meant that it was easier for them to fully engage with what they had done. When they had understood the reasons for themselves, the professionals then looked at how they could help them in the future.

This is so different from a traditional approach in the legal system, where young people are often viewed as objects that do not have the right to be heard or given an explanation. Restorative justice gives these young people the chance to be heard, people can then hear what the issues are and do something about it!

Throughout the process the young people were made to feel they were valued. Yes, they had made a mistake, but that did not mean they did not have amazing qualities. This focus allowed the young people to identify themselves by their strengths and not by the mistakes they had made. It would be great if wider society could see them like this too.

What is significant about this process is that there is a clear understanding of the nature of the roles of the parties who are attending and a clear set of what characteristics or attributes are being encouraged within a conferencing session.

Other settings

Using characteristics or attributes as a focus for the opportunities that you develop can have application in many other spaces too.

We did a piece of work around dental health. The idea here was to encourage children's engagement in the way in which they viewed their dental care; we wanted them to be more involved.

A key starting point in shaping this work was to have a sense of what characteristics we were attaching to children within the context of this setting and this project. These were very simple and suggested that children should:

- have a voice – feel confident to talk and discus their dental health

- be curious – ask questions and find out more

- take responsibility – share strategies for managing their dental health.

We simply created an activity sheet that, in a fun way, encouraged children to think about basic aspects of their dental care while they were waiting to have their teeth checked. These activities could then be shared with the dentist when they were called, breaking down those barriers between professional and child, giving the child a voice to explore any particular questions that they had about their teeth.

The characteristics provided a focus for how we saw the child and, as a result, this then influenced the opportunities or practices that were designed as part of the project.

Reflection

Consider the characteristics that you would like to see children developing in the setting you are part of. Make sure these are clearly connected to the understanding and ideas that we have explored over the last couple of chapters. How do these reflect our ambition for children:

- to establish a voice?

- for that voice to be amplified?

Then discuss your thoughts with children and see what they can add.

ACTION 12: DEVELOP A TECHNICAL VOCABULARY

Having set out the characteristics and the focus that provides, it is important now to consider a language for those vehicles or strategies you are to use in allowing the characteristics to be an explicit part of your engagement with children. The discussions below will introduce a language in relation to:

- participation

- research

- emotions.

Note: In practice there would be value in having a statement that sets out your position in relation to these areas – making that language clear, visible and explicit. This will be encouraged as the section develops.

Defining participation

An intriguing reflection from the academic research is that those in English-speaking countries face an additional challenge when talking about participation. This is because the language itself is restricted – it lacks words that reflect or refer to the variety of ways in which people might 'participate'. This is in contrast to other areas of the world where there are many words that can be used to represent the different parts of the process of children getting involved.

The variety of actions represented in other languages around participation, for example, reflect more strongly the sense that participation is a shared activity (see Savyasaachi and Butler 2014). These words from India (in hindi) highlight a greater range of terms for describing aspects of participation:

Bahgidari – to share and be included

Joodna – to become part of

Sahbhagita – to be co-partners

Sharkat – to be present and be involved in

Seva – to be available

Yogdan – to gift work. (Savyasaachi and Butler 2014, p.50)

South African culture also reflects the importance of participation in shaping the wider community. The term 'ubanta' refers to that sense of interdependence that is so strong in South African culture: 'I am what I am because of who we all are.'

Examples from other places in the world highlight the celebratory nature of people coming together. In Brazil, the Portuguese word 'mutirão' is defined to refer to coming together, but also to the value that shared work holds for that time and place. The depth of meaning that surrounds these words shows their importance to the community in a context where the significance of shared endeavours is recognised as contributing to the good of society as a whole.

The richness of the language of participation in other countries and cultures should challenge us to think carefully about what we mean when we talk about 'participation' in the spaces that we share with children.

The discussions below are there to offer you some ideas that you might wish to draw on to support the way you seek to define participation.

A language of rights

The United Nations Convention on the Rights of the Child (UNCRC) has become the bedrock of a vocabulary for engaging with children for many. For example, it is a driving force for international charities. Indeed, in the case of organisations such as Save the Children they have taken the original articles from the Convention and re-applied these in a practical way, with significant weight on the importance of participation.

If you have not seen the convention it is worth having a look at:

- Adult: www.ohchr.org/EN/ProfessionalInterest/Pages/CRC.aspx

- Child friendly: www.unicef.org/rightsite/files/uncrcc hilldfriendlylanguage.pdf.

The overriding focus for the Convention is protection and provision (as discussed earlier). This has meant that the

Convention can too often become a tool for adults rather than for children. But within the convention there is also a definite recognition of the place for children's participation. For some, this is encouragement enough and Article 12 has become a talisman for action.

Article 12

1. States Parties shall assure to the child who is capable of forming his or her own views *the right to express those views freely in all matters affecting the child*, the views of the child being given due weight in accordance with the age and maturity of the child.

2. For this purpose, the child shall in particular be provided the *opportunity to be heard in any judicial and administrative proceedings affecting the child*, either directly, or through a representative or an appropriate body, in a manner consistent with the procedural rules of national law.

Note: In the context of the arguments in this book, this full extract highlights the restrictions that are placed on children's voices; however, it is the more positive aspects (in italic) that those who favour children's rights rely on.

However, a key problem, mentioned earlier, is that not enough children know about the Convention and, notably, it does not apply in the US. Some have reported how the Convention is better known in emerging countries compared with those countries that are more economically stable. However, if the Convention were shared more, maybe it could come to offer a common language between children, allowing voices to be heard more effectively around the world.

In its most basic form the Convention deals with:

- *Personal rights:* the right to life, to be protected from harm, to be protected from discrimination, to be taken seriously

- *Family and home:* the right to a home, not to suffer harm or neglect

- *School and work*: the right to an education, not to do harmful work

- *Community and environment*: the right to meet with friends, to grow up healthy, to be protected from war, to special protection if you are a refugee.

For many adults 'rights' are seen as a threat. They are a tool that children can use to simply pursue a selfish agenda. However, this misses the point that in claiming a right we are also naturally called to respect that right for others. It is the relationship between rights and a natural responsibility to ensure that others have this right too that makes a language of rights such a useful tool in exploring opportunities within a culture of advocacy.

That international dimension has recently been reinforced through a UN call for children to be seen as Active Citizens, as encouraged by the Education2030 goals that grew out of the eight Millennium Goals. At the centre of UNESCO's drive for 2030 (UNESCO 2016), in conjunction with efforts to combat climate change, is a vision for sustainability, one, they suggest, that can only work if children grow in awareness of their potential and, as part of this, their realisation of how their actions can impact on others.

The Convention is useful, but if we are to create an international language of rights then, as Lundy (2007) suggests, we need to consider a more practical application. If, therefore, you are using a rights-based language, you might wish to assess its application in light of these four criteria:

Space: children must be given opportunity to express views

Voice: children must be facilitated to express views

Audience: the views must be listened to

Influence: the views must be acted up, as appropriate. (Lundy 2007, p.933)

Note: A practical guide to a rights-based approach:
Getting it Right for Children: A practitioner's guide to child rights programming (Save the Children 2007)

Save the Children have provided significant direction to others in how a language of rights can form part of the way we engage with children. This document, and there are many others available online, provides a very practical example for how a rights-based language can offer organisations a framework for action and evaluation.

A language of participation

What the rights model does not do is include a vocabulary that can support groups and organisations which are considering the process of participation. This is addressed in two models below (although there are others).

Hart's model

Roger Hart's ladder (developed in 1992) has been tremendously influential globally in providing a focus on children's participation. It was driven by the vision of Hart to see the value in children's voices and the part they can play in adding richness to the democratic process. Hart challenged the traditional way in which politics is often addressed, with children being asked to simply discuss the top political media story of the day. With this in mind he comments:

> what a wasted opportunity. They [children] should be having elections about things that they know lots about, namely their own lives and the lives of their schools, real democracy... This mock democracy, mock elections, it's a way of playing safe, to avoid getting into some of the tricky and morally challenging issues of local politics that one faces a genuine democratic process. I suppose much of the problem is that in the U.S., we have come to think of democracy as electoral representation. While the nation loudly proclaims itself as a democratic model for the world, it has in fact lost touch with its democratic

origins – with the idea of each person having a voice. (Hart and Schwab 1997, p.177)

It is that sense of engagement that therefore sits behind Hart's ladder. The ladder focuses on types of practice – that would lead only to particular types of opportunities – within organisations.

Pros: A useful model that challenges practitioners to question the approach taken within their organisation.

Cons: Too hierarchical. For some it does not give a sense of children and adults working together. Seen as too one-dimensional and thus limited in the scope through which it can add to the way in which practice comes to be done. As a basic tool to reflect on participation it works, but it is less effective in exploring some of the wider questions. This is a stronger focus in the model overleaf.

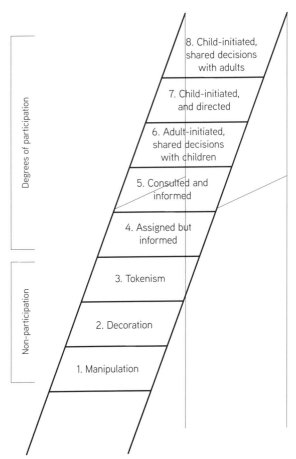

(Source: Hart 1992, p.8)

SHIER'S MODEL
Harry Shier is another important figure that has influenced thinking on children's participation. He is the founder of Cesesma (discussed again later) and, as with Hart, is driven by creating opportunities for children's participation (through amplifying their voice) that are relevant to them and which might play a part in shaping their everyday lives.

Levels of Participation		Openings		Opportunities		Obligations
Children share power and responsibility for decision making		Are you ready to share some of your adult power with children?	→	Is there a procedure that enabled children and adults to share power and responsibility for decisions?	→	Is it a policy requirement that children and adults share power and responsibility for decisions?
			←			
Children are involved in decision making		Are you ready to let children join in your decision making processes?	→	Is there a procedure that enabled children to join in decision-making processes?	→	Is it a policy requirement that children must be involved in decision making processes?
			←	This point is the minimum you must achieve if you endorse the UN Convention on the Rights of the Child	←	
Children's views are taken into account		Are you ready to take children's views into account?	→	Does your decision making process enable you to take children's views into account?	→	Is it a policy requirement that children's views must be given due weight in decision making?
			←			
Children are supported in expressing their views		Are you ready to support children in expressing their views?	→	Do you have a range of ideas and activities to help children express their views?	→	Is it a policy requirement that children must be supported in expressing their views?
			←			
Children are listened to		Are you ready to listen to children?	→	Do you work in a way that enables you to listen to children?	→	Is it a policy requirement that children must be listened to?

(Source: Shier 2001, p.111)

In a practical context Shier's pathways offer groups and organisations an action-driven guide through which to make visible a defined language for children's engagement. It is a model that clearly highlights establishing the voice of the child and encourages consideration of how that might then form part of practice. As a model it is has an organisational focus which means that it is harder to apply to those informal spaces and opportunities where advocacy, in the context of this book, is also seen as having great value. That said, it offers a really useful start.

Reflection

All these models offer tools that might form part of the framework that you adopt. In the context of a culture of advocacy it is important that you are clear about how these processes establish children's voices and then allow them to be amplified – and how within the different steps children are able to demonstrate the attributes highlighted earlier.

- Think about which model you might like to use. Where might you test it out?

- How could you adapt this to ensure that the opportunities you create pursue the attributes or characteristics that you have identified?

Defining research

Research techniques offer a useful way to engage with children's voices.

These techniques should not be seen as the sole preserve of those at a university; rather, they offer tools that can be of great value in building a culture of advocacy and allowing children's voices to be heard.

This section offers an introduction to research. It will give you enough information from which to start building a vocabulary so that you can make use of these techniques within the settings that you share with children. Ultimately what these techniques will allow is for you to think about children as researchers in their own right.

Hearing from children
Speaking to children is the key to advancing a culture of advocacy!

You do not need to read and understand all that is below to speak to children more. What the ideas might offer are ways that you can develop your practices and make more of those conversations.

As suggested above, research should not be confined to formal pieces of work conducted within an academic institution. Rather, the techniques can be useful in helping explore children's voices in a range of settings. For example, what do children think of the food they eat at school or what ideas do they have for the layout of a new shopping mall? What a research approach does is give value to children's voices. It lets children know that what they think counts.

Case study: Museums

Who are museums for? Many museums have exhibits for children but to what extent have children been involved in shaping the nature of that exhibit, the journey that a visitor takes and the experience they have? Some museums have embraced the idea that children can make a significant contribution to how they connect with their visitors, but not all.

Researching assumptions: A group of my university students explored some of these issues in relation to their local museum.

- So much of the process was driven by finding out what it was within the museum that the children found interesting. It is so easy to assume that the toy village section, where children can drive around on cars, is going to be more interesting than the historical section with local artefacts.

- To what extent do the 'don't touch' signs impact on how children engage with the space?

- What do they think of the museum staff – are they there to control them or to interact with them?

In asking these questions, the key was not to assume. Without finding out what children's experiences were actually like, one could not begin to consider how things might change for the better.

Challenging assumptions: What was notable in this small piece of research was the barriers that the adults at the museum presented. It highlighted how important it is that an approach like this is not seen as a judgement on an organisation but rather as an opportunity for conversation and development. Trust is essential as all parties (including the children) feel they have a shared objective in maximising the relevance of a common space.

By drawing from the academic discussions around children and research we can develop the language that we use to talk about it, so that we can make research an active part of the way in which we invite children to share their voices in the variety of settings we work in.

It is therefore useful to consider three key areas (which although they interlink will be introduced separately) which reflect key principles to guide our conversations with children (Frankel 2015). Whether these conversations form part of a large piece of research or a simple chat, these principles will allow us to establish a greater sense of partnership. They are:

- ethics

- communication

- co-operation.

Ethics

Invite children to take part – seek their consent.

As academics have argued, an ethical approach is not only there to protect the child, but, importantly, allows for more effective participation (Roberts-Holmes 2005). The bottom line is that if we wish to establish the voice of the child, and for this voice to be authentic, then it is necessary that we engage in an ethical process.

An ethical process demands that we reflect on the role that we wish children to play and this automatically takes us back to those images of the child that we looked at in Step 1. As we seek to engage with the voice of the child, what statement can we make through the way we 'invite' children to take part? Indeed, it is possible to frame this invitation (through embracing an ethical approach) so that it makes clear:

- the child's importance as an individual

- their capacity to share a view

- their value as a participant (co-constructing the space around them).

Our invitation must therefore allow children to know they have been asked because:

- their voice (as an individual) is important

- they, and only they, have information that would be valuable for furthering understanding

- they are part of the solution.

Notably, this invitation *is* an invitation. It is a request to take part, not an order! As such, through seeking consent, both the nature of this relationship and the role that children are being asked to play can be effectively set.

Consent

The issue of consent must be at the centre of framing your efforts to gather children's voices.

Consent is key because it makes a statement about partnership and the role that the child is expected to play. Indeed the protocols that are adopted can firmly establish the commitment to working together effectively. Consent should be driven by a desire to create experiences, not by assumptions about children's age. Some things to consider, as part of a framework to guide consent, include:

- the child's permission

- parent permission/gatekeeper permission

- immediate withdrawal (child can pull out whenever they want)

- the child has understanding of the reason for the research and how the data will be used

- the data will be kept anonymous

- research will be sensitive to children's needs (including suitable surroundings)

- child protection: make your position on this clear – for example, children are made aware that, although the research is anonymous, should anything emerge that causes the researcher concern then they will need to share that with other adults (see Alderson 1995, Butler 2012).

Building consent – an important lesson that we can learn from academic work is the importance of recognising that consent might be something to be worked at. In areas where children's voices have not regularly been collected or engaged with, it might take a little more work to establish consent. The point is that this is okay.

Also, it is important that any limitations to the child's ability to communicate are not seen as a hindrance to pursuing their consent. It might just mean exploring a range of relevant alternatives. For example, if children are unable to write their name they may wish to do a hand or thumbprint or even to draw a self portrait (see Butler 2012).

As you seek to explore consent and invite children's participation in any research, you may look to use:

- conversations

- information leaflets

- posters

- questions and answers

- personal invitations (cards).

Communication
GETTING THE QUESTION RIGHT!
Make sure that children know what they are being asked!

If you ask a question that the children you are working with don't understand, then the research is of little value (other than to show they don't understand the question!). It is therefore important that we do not assume that the language we might use to frame the question is right. We need to check this out. In fact, getting it wrong should not be seen as a failure but simply as part of the process.

In practice, as you think about communication and the way in which you seek to ask your questions this might mean:

- piloting and testing approaches to encouraging children's voices

- working with children to develop a shared vocabulary that allows them to engage with the themes within the research.

CASE STUDY

Some very prominent theories around children were based on research that was conducted in a laboratory (Piaget 1975[1935]). The questions that were asked were developed by the researcher and the responses came to be seen as a universal explanation of children's thinking. It was great that children were being spoken to, however what was not so effective was the context and the way in which the questions were asked. When later researchers tried to ask the same questions, this time using puppets, they got a different response. It was concluded that the use of puppets allowed the children to connect more clearly with what they were being asked, which obviously then shaped their answers (Donaldson and McGarrigle 1975).

Getting the questions right – so that they are relevant and accessible – is key.

You may work somewhere like a shopping centre where your experience of directly engaging with children might be limited; this should not restrict your ambition to ask questions. However, you might not know what the right question to ask is. Invite children to attend a focus group. Tell them about the project and invite their input. Share the questions you wish to ask and explore with them how they might respond and whether the questions could be asked in any other way. Use this feedback to inform a further conversation, or you may be ready to just start asking your questions!

CREATING YOUR OWN QUESTIONS

Knowing who you are asking the questions to and how you are asking the questions, and how you are going to process your data (see the next section) is going to frame the type of question that you ask. However try to:

- keep the questions simple

- make sure they allow you to find out something you really want to know

- as much as possible, present your question so children are excited about answering it (engagement is essential)

- run a pilot – test your ideas out.

Note: The best way to develop your questioning or encourage children to develop their questioning is to practice. Have a go, make mistakes, try again and you will build up your ability to work with children to ask the right questions that allow their voices to be heard.

Co-operation
Whereas communication was about the question, 'co-operation' is about the questioning.

PARTNERSHIP
Co-operation is about ensuring a partnership between researcher and participant that allows for maximum engagement, which will in turn make the data collected more authentic.

It means considering:

- how children are approached – that initial introduction to the research

- the way the research is conducted – the methods that you pick

- how, where relevant and possible, children are informed about the results of that research.

Being a male researcher is something that I often reflect on. Sometimes this means that I have to go to greater efforts to break down any perceived power barriers that the children might have when talking to me. This means, in the context of a school, for example, always being known by my first name, never wearing a tie and seeing whether I can come up with some kind of opening exercise that is very different to what they might do in the classroom.

ASKING YOUR QUESTIONS

Resource Sheet 5 provides some examples of some simple methods you might wish to use (the table reflects a chart that we use with children). All of these approaches are just as relevant in an adult context; however, the key to making this work with children lies both in the nature of the question asked and in how the question is asked. It means that an adult and child questionnaire will be two very different things, shaped by the accessibility of language, the style of questioning and the nature of the approach, although they may collect similar types of data.

ANALYSIS

As you think about how you will go about your questioning you will also need to think about how you are going to collect and analyse your data. Of course there are layers to analysis. However, the level of analysis you offer can simply be based on the experience you have. If you are just beginning – first you might want to simply find out if children enjoy, for example, their visit to the museum (with a questionnaire using closed questions that allow you to build up frequencies of particular responses). Second, after building up some confidence, you might then ask why (running some focus groups in which children talk about their experiences and you record the conversation and draw elements out from it).

Note: The analysis you offer should not be presented as anything more than what it is, that is, a representation of some voices from some children at a certain time, based on the questions that were asked.

Children as researchers

Although the previous section might have been written as if it were just for adults undertaking research, all the information forms part of a programme we use with children as we support them to become a team of researchers.

Adults asking the questions is useful and can be an important starting point. However, children asking the questions themselves can be incredibly powerful. Research teams can be supported by adults to:

- decide the nature and type of their questions
- how they are going to ask them
- capture and interrogate the data
- present the analysis.

An inspirational project that shows the potential of children as researchers is Cesesma.[1] Here, children from rural Nicaragua have been trained up to run their own research projects, allowing them to ask questions about issues that are important to their everyday lives. These projects not only allow children to have a voice, but their data has offered them a platform to share their findings more widely – leading to change.

Connecting to emotions

If children are to be effectively engaged in a process where their voice is valued, then it is important that they feel confident and comfortable about sharing in the first place. An initial step is to give children confidence to talk about their emotions and to share how they are feeling.

Reference has already been made to this in Chapter 1. The point here is that children sometimes don't have the language to effectively share what they are feeling. Those feelings then come to be displayed in other ways; for example, through their actions.

---

1   www.cesesma.org

In order for children to be in a position to confidently share their voice it is necessary for them to have a language (in whatever form that might be) for addressing the following:

- I am (being able to describe oneself)

- You are (having words to recognise and describe others)

- I feel (to recognise and share one's feelings)

- You feel (to recognise and to communicate the feelings of others).

There is obviously a significant amount of depth in the skills involved in exploring emotions, as children look to not only interpret how they are feeling inside but then look to be able to identify that in others.

CASE STUDIES

Finding a shared vocabulary

The importance of being able to talk about emotions was illustrated in a recent visit my colleague, John Fowler, made to Australia. Here, he was working with an aboriginal community where attendance at school was really low. One of the reasons for this was that the children were not able to talk about and discuss how they felt. This then created a barrier to their learning and to any form of self expression or to children being able to share their voice effectively.

The problem was intensified by the fact that within white Australian culture and aboriginal culture the language used to talk about emotions was very different. What emerged was that the aboriginal children needed a different type of vocabulary – one that was in line with their culture. So a language for emotional engagement grew out of the way in which the children talked about the weather. Here are some examples. What was significant was that simply by being able to talk about their emotions, the children realised that they had a place in school and attendance increased in a remarkably short space of time.

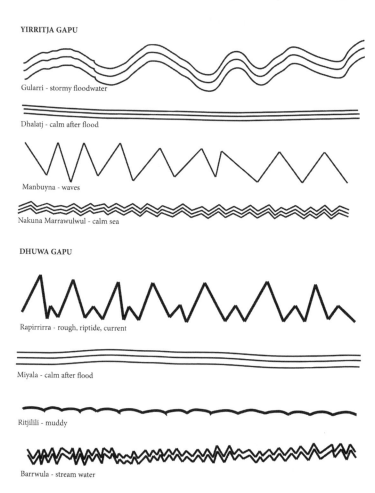

YIRRITJA GAPU

Gularri - stormy floodwater

Dhalatj - calm after flood

Manbuyna - waves

Nakuna Marrawulwul - calm sea

DHUWA GAPU

Rapirrirra - rough, riptide, current

Miyala - calm after flood

Ritjilili - muddy

Barrwula - stream water

Natural water patterns as an emotional category

Having a voice will be influenced, as suggested earlier, to some extent by how we think about or feel about ourselves and those around us. If can, therefore, be a very important step to allow or support children to express their feelings as part of releasing their voice (see also Action 13).

Talking about feelings

A very simple activity that we have run to find out what children think about sharing their feelings involved asking a small group (four children) just two questions:

- Are children good at sharing their feelings?

- Should children share their feelings and why?

Of course the 'why' is really important. What this activity has shown is the extent to which children reflect on the nature of the space and how they feel towards those within it before they decide what they share about how they are feeling. Sometimes, therefore, it might not be an issue with language that impacts on an ability to express oneself, but a concern about how others in the space will react ('because sometimes they don't feel comfortable', 'it helps the adults to understand', 'because it will help you').

The fear of sharing your emotions can be very real. In one piece of work we invited a small number of children who were finding school hard to be part of a group. The idea of the group was to give them a chance to talk, to share their thoughts and feelings. However, the first step was to simply get them to talk about themselves. Low self esteem meant that when we asked these children to share something positive about themselves they found it hard. So instead we asked the other children to do this on behalf of each other. Each week the children would share something positive about one of the others in the group. Not only did it help them develop their language but it also helped them to grow in confidence as they began to recognise the positive ways in which they could contribute to school life.

Reflection

Have a think about a project that you could run to explore how children feel about sharing their emotions.

CONCLUSION

Language is key to unlocking children's ability to engage and allow their voices to be heard. Step 3 has introduced the way in which language can be used to form a focus by developing a set of attributes or characteristics, but also the extent to which it is important to think about a more technical language that can help to bring these characteristics alive. This was encouraged through sections on:

- participation
- research
- connecting with emotions.

All of these sections reflect on tools and methods that you can draw on in different ways to help you to facilitate a culture of advocacy. Participation is not going to be effective unless people within your setting know what participation is. The models in this section can therefore be used to help in a very practical way.

All of these techniques need to be tested out. You will need to tweak them and shape them so that they are of use to you and the children that you work with.

So give things a go and see what works. The key message in this chapter is: if you can define what you are talking about, it does make a difference. Use a language that both you and the children understand within your setting; this will open up the space for really effective engagement and will give both you and the children the confidence you need so that voices can be heard and understood!

CREATING OPPORTUNITIES

	Steps	
Part 1: Creating a climate for change	Step 1 – Revitalise your thinking!	
	Step 2 – Be Spatially Aware	
Part 2: Turning rhetoric into reality	Step 3 – Speak the right language	
	Step 4 – Create opportunities	13. Build opportunities that encourage the individual
		14. Create opportunities that are relevant
		15. Design opportunities that empower
		16. Be ambitious in how these opportunities can offer change
Section objectives	• Understand the key ingredients to effective opportunities.	
	• Be able to put the opportunity framework into practice.	
	• Feel confident in creating opportunities that can have a positive impact.	

Unless there is an intention to create opportunities for action, the effort of reading the previous pages has been wasted. The effectiveness of a culture of advocacy will be defined in terms of its ability to increase children's participation and, as a result, inform change. As adults, simply having a change in attitude towards children (as encouraged in Part 1) is not enough, children need both an opportunity to share their voice and a platform from which that voice can be heard, turning thought into action, rhetoric into reality.

A culture of advocacy has been defined as an ambition to:

- establish the child's voice: children's voices are acknowledged and valued

- amplify the child's voice: opportunities are created that allow children's voices to be heard, giving others the chance to respond or engage.

Here, therefore, we begin to focus on what this might look like in practice as we consider some underlying ingredients that, if we are mindful of them, will help to shape opportunities so that they allow the voice of the child to emerge and then give it a basis on which it can be shared, informing the setting that they are part of.

Establishing a platform for children's voices to be heard is not the difficult part. What is hard is finding a platform that is meaningful and which allows a voice to be shared with the wider community. History is full of examples of children creating their own platforms, as represented through the wearing of particular clothes (hoodies), listening to certain music and engaging in particular activities (tagging). Such platforms are seen as counter cultural, as deviant even, as they reflect the voices of a disenfranchised group that can't see any other way to express themselves.

This approach is about creating opportunities for action that include adults and children and that establish a basis through which both can be part of shaping and defining a community, in which all voices are valued.

CREATING OPPORTUNITIES

CASE STUDY: A cautionary tale

It was 2003 and the UK government had outlined its intention to fight a war in Iraq (Cunningham and Lavalette 2004). There was significant public disquiet. One outstanding intervention in the public debate came from school children in the form of school strikes. As one columnist notes:

> This spring, in the first days of war with Iraq, the country was witness to a new kind of protest. In the most significant child led campaign for a century, school children as young as 10 walked out of their classrooms to attend what were for most, their first political demonstrations...these young people were organising and leading their own protests, leafleting at school gates, organising e-mail networks and expertly working the media. Their determination to be heard was palpable. The results were awesome. (Brooks 2003, p.41)

School strikes took place in the US, Switzerland, Greece, Denmark, Sweden, Italy, Spain, Australia and the UK.

The wider public reacted with surprise to the response of children, both in terms of their actions but also the sophistication of their arguments.

In the UK the strikes were connected by the media to the introduction of citizenship classes in 1998. Notably this connection was a negative one. Citizenship classes were seen as fuelling children's actions, giving children ideas that they should not have. The reaction of those in authority, particularly in the schools themselves, was to deal with the children's actions in the tried and tested manner – through punishment. The children's behaviour was seen as a threat to the accepted order and needed to be controlled!

Herein lies the contradiction. On the one hand, citizenship classes encourage children and young people to show concern for the 'common good', to engage in 'active citizenship' and to accept the consequences of their actions; yet, on the other hand, their 'reward' for proactively articulating their concerns over a major world crisis has been, on the whole, admonishment and ridicule. (Cunningham and Lavalette 2004, p.265)

In many ways this case study sums up the challenge.

Adults are nervous about creating platforms for children because of what the consequences might be. Here, a potentially positive opportunity for engagement was countered with a destructive response that was focused on one main objective, reminding children that adults were in charge.

Here, in Step 4, the aim is to offer some headings that might focus a different approach to creating opportunities for children to engage and for their voice to be heard.

An effective opportunity therefore:

- *encourages* the individual

- *creates* relevant experiences

- *empowers* children as change makers

- is *ambitious* in scope and intended outcomes.

The effectiveness of opportunities based around these headings will be linked directly to those themes around language that we considered in Step 3.

The table below offers a practical tool to assess opportunities (see Resource Sheet 6). Supporting detail is provided in the following pages.

What is the setting?			
Who is going to be involved in this opportunity?			
What characteristics/attributes would you like children to experience as part of this opportunity?			
What is this opportunity?			
This opportunity/ platform	How is this visible?	How might this be added to?	Your action steps
Encourages the individual			
Creates relevant experiences			
Empowers children as change makers			
Is ambitious in scope and intended outcomes			

ACTION 13: AN OPPORTUNITY *ENCOURAGES* THE INDIVIDUAL

A culture of advocacy is driven by a desire to increase the way in which children come to value their voice.

Taking part in advocacy must, therefore, increasingly be recognised for the positive impact it has on the individual child. Research reflects the connection between children's engagement with their voice through the opportunity to use it in a meaningful way and the positive development of their self identity. One academic (Honneth 1995) identifies three criteria in the development of identity:

- self confidence – the ability to express your needs and wants (a willingness to share ideas)

- self respect – having a sense of yourself as a person (a sense of purpose)

- self esteem – recognising in your uniqueness what makes you feel valuable (sense of value in your contribution).

These criteria provide a useful focus for the creation of an effective opportunity or platform, as they encourage the individual and allow them to develop a sense of personal worth. Step 1 highlighted the extent to which the history of advocacy reflects past efforts to disconnect certain groups from a sense of personal value as a way of excluding their voice from society; it is therefore important that any opportunities that are created encourage children to value their input. Academic Tom Cockburn writes:

> For children, hearing their voices or accessing their views, experiences, dreams, fears, desires and uncertainties holds out the possibility for children to discover and negotiate the essence of who they are and their place in the world. (2013, pp.221–222)

Opportunity to be assessed (from example – school council meetings)			
	How encouraged	How displayed	Recommendations
Self confidence (willingness to share ideas)			
Self respect (sense of purpose – you are meant to be there)			
Self esteem (sense of value – you can make a particular contribution)			

It is important to note that step between how an action is encouraged and then how that comes to be displayed. This should be part of an ongoing process of reflection as one seeks to make the most of an opportunity that encourages children to learn to value who they are and the role that they play in the world around them.

Recognising the value of one's voice is essential. The table (see Resource Sheet 7) above offers a tool through which you can start to interrogate an opportunity and to consider how it 'encourages' the individual, as you examine, self-confidence, self-respect and self-esteem.

Reflection

- Where do you feel the voice of the child has yet to be established and what opportunities might change this?

- Identify an activity that you could test out the table above on. Then try it.

  - How did it change the nature of the opportunity?

ACTION 14: AN OPPORTUNITY *CREATING* RELEVANT EXPERIENCES
Making opportunities meaningful

Perhaps the best example of the traditional platform for advocacy is the formal setting of a courtroom. Here, a defined set of processes, based on particular roles, frames and shapes the nature of the opportunity that is created. The problem with this as noted by Cockburn (2013) in his analysis of the work of Mayo and Rooke (2008), is that, 'Young people are less likely to express themselves in more formal contexts, and only a few feel they can do this meaningfully' (Cockbum 2013, p.217). A reason for this is that these 'opportunities' are not relevant.

The aim here is to consider *creating* more informal platforms for advocacy, ones that are relevant as they offer opportunities for children to share their voices, building learning experiences. It is important for us as adults to recognise the value of the opportunity itself. Nineteenth-century English philosopher John Stuart Mill, in his musings on the democratic process, wrote:

> we do not learn to read or write, or ride or swim, by being merely told how to do it, but by doing it, so it is only by practicing popular government on a limited scale, that the people learn how to exercise it on a larger scale. (cited in Cockburn 2014, p.213)

Although Mill had his doubts about the ability of children, in keeping with many others at the time, the sentiment here offers us an interesting point for reflection as it encourages us to *create* opportunities. If we wish children to develop their ability to further the democratic system, then they need the chance to experience it. They need opportunities that are relevant to developing their democratic potential. The point here can easily be stretched more widely in the context of advocacy. If we wish children to establish a voice and to amplify that voice, then we as adults need to give them 'relevant' opportunities.

In relation to democracy, therefore, the starting point must not be seen as one's first vote at the age of 18. Rather, as adults, we need to be more creative in establishing those relevant opportunities so that one's experience of democracy builds on a variety of opportunities that prepare one to vote in the future, but more importantly encourage engagement in the present.

A culture of advocacy is therefore about *creating* opportunities in which children can explore and test out their skills and how they can use their voice most effectively.

In developing opportunities that are relevant and creative, don't forget the need to speak to children.

Informal platforms

Advocacy cannot be seen as restricted to particular settings. An informal platform in the home offers plenty of scope for creating relevant opportunities, in the same way as school and other settings. Indeed, merely creating opportunities for conversation can be of great value.

These informal platforms are just as important as the more definable formal platforms. It is often easier to make such opportunities of particular personal relevance. Here the skilled role of adults as facilitators re-emerges – a theme that will be considered in more detail in Step 5.

CASE STUDY: Creating a shared online space

Yes, children can create opportunities alone. However, adults and children can also create opportunities together.

The internet provides an opportunity for children to have a voice and to share it. The phenomena of YouTube fame for video diarists, the 'vloggers', and their interest for children and young people, reflects this. The issue is that adults have one perception of the internet and often children have another. Rather than the internet developing as a co-constructed platform, it becomes an adult-free space that children seek to figure out on their own. The danger is that without the opportunities to practice and develop one's skills, there is a range of potential risks. The biggest threat is that once something is written, it can't be unwritten. For many, the internet can thus become a space that is not dissimilar to the tightrope walker choosing to practice without a safety net.

On the other hand the internet can be a fantastic space through which children can share. The international profile of Syrian girl Bana is just such an example (@alabedbana). Here, Bana's mother worked with her to establish the site and clearly plays a very active role in supporting her daughter in sharing her thoughts. (Of course Malala Yousefzi's story started in a similar way.)

Some might argue that adults' involvement damages the authenticity of the child's voice – and it can – but the point is that, working together, adults and children can create relevant platforms that not only allow their voices to be heard, but allow children to grow in their expertise as advocates.

The word 'create' in the heading for this section is intentional. For the most relevant opportunities are those that are constructed by adults and children building together. Talking to each other as the pieces are put in place to establish a platform not only allows for children's voices to be shared, but also provides the chance for them to build and develop their understanding and their role in a culture of advocacy.

Note: Language is of course very influential for creating opportunities that are relevant. This was a particular theme in Step 3, in relation to the attributes or characteristics that we might associate with children in our setting and the more technical language we might use to develop relevant opportunities, particularly the discussion around research and the importance of asking the right questions in the right way!

Reflection

- Create some ideas for opportunities where no opportunity has been before.

- How will you make this relevant?

- What learning experience are you keen to encourage?

ACTION 15: AN OPPORTUNITY *EMPOWERS* CHILDREN AS CHANGE MAKERS

Opportunities should engage with children as agents of change.

The mass of research that has taken place around participation since the 1960s shows that the most fruitful conditions for transformation are created when the process builds from the bottom up, as communities become empowered.

Top down does not work

Since the 1960s and 1970s there has been growing engagement with the notion of participation. As such this new definable participation became directly connected to social movements as they focused increasingly on models that rejected the direct link between outside help or instruction and 'change', and instead concentrated on empowering local people and through this allowed real change to take place.

These thoughts on participation were initially linked to international development work, and people such as Paulo Freire were among the first to present models of empowerment where local people were acknowledged as part of bringing that change about (for more see www.freire.org).

This meant some important shifts. At the centre of this was the extent to which the individual within their community must be:

- given the chance to talk and be listened to

- taken seriously

- part of shaping a response.

What is particularly powerful about this model is the extent to which real change was the result of engaging with those people for whom the change mattered. It was about empowering the people who would traditionally have been at the bottom of a ladder of support to realise that they are the key to improving outcomes. A bottom-up approach meant that the voices of those that were most likely to be excluded actually became a central ingredient to building change (Chambers 1983).

CASE STUDY

This case study is from Madison Eckert (a former student of mine and a community worker).

A mum of five children cannot send all her children to school with food one day. She decides to keep them at home because she fears if they were at school a teacher might notice and report her to social workers. Surely they would just help her out? But she believes her voice will not be heard and it will be left to others to make assumptions about her and her family. Whether it is this mum or some of the young people I know who live in this particular neighbourhood, which is full of challenges, all are wary of the outsider and any ideas they might have.

Working in these communities I have learnt from experience that trying to 'tell' people what they need to do, will not work. In fact, this approach just misses the point. If I want to be any help, what is most important is trust. But to build trust you need time, time to listen. What has struck me most is that by listening you start to find out the amazing ideas that already exist in these communities. Let's go back to the mum I mentioned earlier. She had an idea. She just needed some encouragement. The idea was simple, instead of mums worrying about sending children to school with no food – she would, through inspiring others ensure there were food baskets at school that the children could make use of. Would this idea have been successful if it had been suggested by someone from outside? I don't know, but it is likely it would not have been *as* successful. Knowing the food was provided by other mums who knew the issues parents without food faced, made the difference. Allowing someone to use their voice in the neighbourhood is empowering. And who better to put ideas into practice than those who truly understand the needs.

What this example shows is that a sense of empowerment is not the result of a top-down policy driven by the local council. Rather, here, empowerment and the opportunity to share one's voice came in the informal and modest act of someone who understood the need simply offering baskets of food.

It presents us with a significant challenge. If we are to create a culture of advocacy the opportunities we offer need to empower children to recognise that they are the fundamental ingredient to any change. Our practices as adults therefore need to focus on ways in which children are empowered and given the opportunities to shape and direct that change as we ask (using the ideas above):

- are children being given the chance to talk – to identify the issues

- are they being taken seriously

- are children being invited to help form the response to what has been heard?

As we therefore assess our opportunities we might wish to consider the nature and type of participation that we are offering to children. Is it:

1. Nominal participation – for display – top down

2. Instrumental participation – focused on particular end, top down may consult

3. Representative participation – bottom up, but driven by interests and focus of those at top

4. Transformational participation – participation both means and end for top and bottom – aim is empowerment. (White 1996)

In the world of international development the move towards transformational participation has been strong. Today, we need to look at those same principles in shaping domestic opportunities for children to participate in their everyday lives. Transformational participation will empower children to recognise the value of their voice and then to act on it.

Note: The tables that explored a language for participation in Step 3 should be applied here (see Resource Sheet 3). They will allow you to assess the extent to which your project builds from the bottom up, giving you a language to challenge and change as required. Also you may be interested to find out more about techniques used to support a bottom-up approach – for example, an influential international development approach called 'Participatory Rural Appraisal' or PRA.

CASE STUDY: Power

A simple way in which children can be empowered is through challenging traditional barriers around power. Children are used to being part of 'opportunities' in which adults have the power. Indeed, adults are used to this too. What is needed is a way of engagement that encourages mutuality and a sense of partnership. Through this a sense of empowerment will flow.

You might therefore want to consider the nature or type of relationship that you have with children. How would you and the children characterise the nature of the roles and relationship in your setting?

- Powerful: one who has control, can shape and direct the nature of opportunities.

- Powerless: one who follows, accepts and does not question directions.

- Mutual: a true sense of partnership, built on a sense of mutual understanding, respect and trust.

This was explored with a group of children who felt marginalised at school and 'done unto'. They were constantly the focus of adults' measures for control and had a clear sense of the power barriers between them and the staff.

What these children needed was the opportunity to think about themselves as something other than 'powerless'. These children were offered a time to meet – creating their own group outside of the classroom. This forum was theirs to shape. It gave them a chance to speak freely to share their feelings and to regain a sense of control. By challenging that sense that they were always powerless these children were able to start moving towards a more healthy sense of their participation, creating their own ideas to improve life at school.

Reflection

- What themes from this section have stood out to you?

- In what ways might you seek to put some of this into practice?

ACTION 16: AN OPPORTUNITY IS *AMBITIOUS* ABOUT CHANGE

The more doors we open to children's involvement, the more we will see the wider benefits in society.

One of the repetitive themes so far has been the importance of not underestimating children and the role they can play in shaping society. As children's voices are engaged with, we then need to think about the platforms that allow them to be effectively shared, encouraging them to be ambitious about the change their voices might result in.

CASE STUDY: Disability

Disabled children are doubly disadvantaged. They face assumptions for being children and they face assumptions for being disabled.

This raises questions about how these individuals come to be valued within the context of advocacy. Talk around need gets in the way of children having a wider voice and demonstrating their capacity and ambition to participate.

The following student project took place at a horse riding centre for children with disabilities. For the very first time this project gave the children the chance to get involved. Despite complex issues around communication, these children were invited in ways that were relevant to them to share their thoughts. Once these were recorded the team at the centre looked to find ways to put them into practice. For one child this was about making an obstacle challenge for him and his horse to take on. For another it was about being given the opportunity to share his love of art through selling pictures he had drawn as cards through the centre.

These activities were not about changing the world, but they were about changing the experience of the individual children and indeed how the adults around saw them. It needed a set of opportunities that were driven by ambition. There were plenty of barriers that could have got in the way (and some still did), but recognising the power in the opportunity and the extent to which it could bring about some change fuelled activities that made all involved challenge their perspective of the value of children's involvement.

For many, the debate around disability can often focus on need, which can get in the way of hiding the potential an individual has to be involved.

What this case study highlights is that our ambition to promote change should be used to overcome those limitations or restrictions that have surrounded children's voices in the past, with links to Steps 3 and 5.

However it is also important to note here that part of being ambitious is to try things out. Ideas will not always work as you and the children envisaged, but that should not stop you from giving it a go. Although when trying something out it is important to be able to recognise when it is not working and be prepared to say it is time to stop. It then becomes a test run, one you can reflect on and build on in the future.

Note: How we think about change or transformation is important. Rather than seeing this in terms of a list of achievements we must be open to the fact that transformation can be more subtle, as change occurs gradually. The change might not be sudden and defined but constant and evolving. Our ambition for change will develop through partnership with children. It is not necessarily about creating platforms that see their voices shared with 100,000 people but, rather, being ambitious about the impact that it can have on each individual and the relationships that are part of their everyday lives.

Reflection

Reflect on ways in which projects you have been involved with have encouraged a sense of ambition.

In what areas are you keen to be more ambitious?

CONCLUSION

Step 4 has offered four points for consideration as you seek to encourage opportunities for children's voices to be engaged with and then heard, as summed up in the following table (see Resource Sheet 6).

What is the setting?
Who is going to be involved in this opportunity?
What characteristics/attributes would you like children to experience as part of this opportunity?
What is this opportunity?

This opportunity/platform	How is this visible?	How might this be added to?	Your action steps
Encourages the individual			
Creates relevant experiences			
Empowers children as change makers			
Is ambitious in scope and intended outcomes			

The case studies that follow the conclusion look at these headings in the context of two very different settings, showing practical ways in which a context of advocacy takes shape.

CASE STUDIES

Home

One of the most powerful experiences I have had working with parents came in a parenting session when a dedicated and devoted single mum told the group with tears in her eyes that her life had quite literally changed for the better. What had caused this change? For seven years her son had been a part of her life, but only now was she starting to hear him. Parenting, for her, had always been defined by a traditional model in which the parent and the parent alone knows best. It was how she was parented and how her parents were parented. However, it was not working. She was unhappy and her son was unhappy. As part of a parenting course she was introduced to a new image of the child – an image in which the child was actively making sense of what was going on around them, and, importantly, had a view and an opinion that should matter.

She started to think about this and over the next few weeks she began to engage with her child in a different way. Rather than to instruct and direct, she began to ask and, importantly, then make the time to listen to her son's answers. By creating this space they were able to talk about a particular issue that had been damaging their relationship. The son liked to be organised. He wanted to make sure everything was in place before he left for school. Previously mum saw this as her responsibility. She would pack the bag, she would leave for school when she thought it was time, telling him not to worry, that she had it under control. It wasn't that he didn't believe her, it was simply that he just wanted to be sure. He wanted to have some control and be able to manage and take responsibility for going to school. Through conversation they decided to create a checklist. The checklist provided a way for both of them to work through what needed to be done before leaving for school. A simple change, but it had a transformative effect.

Encourage
Sadly the history of parenting does not reflect much ambition to promote children's confidence in their own voice. The Victorian saying 'children should be seen and not heard' continues to play a part in certain parenting techniques. It is not that such parents did not want the best for their child, but more that having a voice was not

seen as part of that journey. The mum in this case study reflects many others whose approach to parenting saw little relevance in what the child had to say. However, as soon as this mum had her initial image of the child challenged, she began to view her son in a very different way. For her, giving her son a sense that his voice mattered was the first step in building opportunities that could impact on their life at home and beyond.

Through the simple process of asking questions and making sure there was time to listen to the answers, the son began to grow in his sense of self confidence, self respect and self esteem.

Create

The connection between our attitude towards the child (the image we hold) and the practices that we employ has been considered before. In this example, a change in attitude led to a change in the types of opportunities that were created.

It highlights that, if we are to create relevant opportunities, it is first important that we challenge our thinking about the child, for the nature of the opportunities that we create and the extent to which they will be seen as relevant will be defined by the 'image of the child' that we hold.

Here a key theme was linked to that time to listen. What mum and son agreed was that the best time for both of them to really concentrate on one another was whilst they were walking home from school. As a result they created a 'platform' from which both were able to share, with the understanding that the other would listen.

A key part of the opportunity to have a voice that was created here was the important conversation around when each of their voices would be most effectively heard. Rather than listening therefore being tokenistic, it became a focused activity – making it relevant to both parties as part of shaping those spaces that they shared.

Empower

A powerful element of this case study is that the solutions here did not lie in the knowledge and direction of an outside agency, but rather were driven as a consequence of the changing attitude of the mum. Here the mum realised that it was her and her son that had the capacity to inform and shape change; they just needed to recognise that potential and then to construct opportunities to bring that change about.

The change for this family was not imposed from outside; rather, the opportunities emerged by empowering the two parties (the mum and the son). However, that sense of empowerment was supported by outside sources. The mum received some training and the school played a part (not mentioned in this case study) in supporting the son. That process of empowerment therefore may initially need outside support or scaffolding until it takes root.

Ambition

Once the mum's attitude towards her son changed, so too did the ambition she had for him and for them. As a result her son was no longer the problem; rather, he was part of the solution. All the practices that developed within this home reflected the mum increasingly recognising the role that her son could play in overcoming the challenges *they* faced. This ambition drove the opportunities that developed as the son increasingly took on responsibility for managing aspects of his day-to-day life (with the support of his mum), with an increasing expectation of the role both could play in creating a 'shared' space (and in developing *their own* sense of a 'common' good).

In the community

The following case study is an example of transformation inspired by the power of children's voices.

South Africa has had an interesting relationship with children. During the years of struggle with apartheid children played a big part in fighting against the segregation of black and white people (the 16th of June each year is 'Youth Day' in South Africa, remembering the role young people played in the Soweto uprising of 1976). Indeed in recognition of this, Nelson Mandela's government nearly caused an international stir by reducing the voting age to 16 to include this clearly politicised section of society. However, standing outside of this global norm was a step too far for this society that was going through so much change. The result was that relationships between adults and children returned to a far more traditional way of thinking, characterised by a clear social hierarchy.

This relationship with children was brought into focus as a result of the severe challenge South Africa faced at the turn of the millennium with HIV, which has had a catastrophic impact on society and on families. Driven by a desire to challenge the negative 'noise' around the child that was emerging in the press, with orphans being linked to school drop out, sex and crime, a project emerged that was focused on giving children back their own voice.

Encourage

The project recognised the positive contribution children could make to their families and society more widely. However it recognised that if it was to encourage children, it would need to stand up to the negative representations that were so overt within the press.

Analyses of South African media reporting critique a tendency to 'use the voices of children' to support preconceived stories rather than to inform the account: 'Children...are enlisted as characters to enrich and confirm the journalist's stake on the situation, rather than brought in as active participants in creating their own representations' (Bird and Rahfaldt 2011, p.54 cited in Meintjes 2014, p.150).

This opportunity needed, therefore, to start by re-evaluating how the voice of the child is valued. Again, its simplicity was the key. Children were trained to conduct interviews. It was therefore not about children standing up and giving a political speech, but simply being encouraged to ask questions about those everyday things that really mattered to them. It was in asking these questions that a platform was created in which the children felt their voice was going to be valued. It was through the process, the activity, of recording that the children were given the important encouragement that was a focus of Action 13.

Create
One stand-out feature of these opportunities was their informal nature. Simply providing the children with a microphone allowed them the chance to engage with subjects that were relevant to them through informal conversations with key adults in their life.

This was a simple yet creative idea, that provided a 'relevant' opportunity for children to have a voice within the context of relationships where it had been difficult to be heard. The use of the microphone as a tool to 'amplify' their voice meant that for, many of these children, they were able to have conversations that they had long thought about but had never expressed in words.

A feature of this opportunity was also the related skills that supported the children in representing their voice, as they grew in their ability to manage a conversation with adults such that both sides could constructively share their thoughts as barriers came down and adults began to consider the importance of creating 'truly' shared spaces.

Empower

What was so special about this activity was the extent to which through asking the questions (very much a bottom-up approach) the children were empowered to advance change in their communities. At the start of this project the relationships between adults and children were not positive. A top-down approach was not likely to change this, as adults were holding onto very set understandings of children. However, as the children asked the questions and as the adults were invited to talk about those issues that were of importance to the children, attitudes started to change.

An example of this was a conversation that one child had with his parents about the selling of his goat. He had not been consulted about his goat being sold and he had been deeply upset by what had happened. No one had ever discussed it with him. However, through the process of his questioning his parents about it they grew in their understanding of their child, of the way in which he had been impacted by this experience and about how they would deal with such an issue in the future.

As one head teacher said in relation to the project as a whole:

> What I have learnt is that we look at kids or think about kids as not being aware of issues, or of issues not affecting them. But after hearing the programs I've realised that children know about things we think they don't know about. I realised that they know, and if given a chance to speak about those things, they speak. I realised that they think deeply about these things and these issues that they raise...I no longer look at children as more children who do not know anything. I look at them as people who

know something and who have something to say to me, and who can speak freely and be just as confident as an adult (Meintjes 2014, p.163)

The result was that this platform had created a means through which this community was empowered, in which it was able to grow together.

Ambition

Yes there was an ambition here to promote social change, but the real change took place in the intimate conversations that children had with adults. Without those 'small' changes, big change was not possible.

For us, simply recognising the fact that if children can have a voice and that voice can be shared, it has the potential to create change which is very powerful. It highlights the ambition in the power of conversation and ultimately in the power of an approach to advocacy that releases children's voices, so that others in a community can benefit from engaging with them.[1]

---

1   Take time to have a look at this project and the interviews the children conducted: www.childrencount.org.za/radio/index.php

LEAD THE CHANGE

	Steps	
Part 1: Creating a climate for change	Step 1 – Revitalise your thinking!	
	Step 2 – Be spatially aware	
Part 2: Turning rhetoric into reality	Step 3 – Speak the right language	
	Step 4 – Create opportunities	
	Step 5: Lead the change	17. Have an idea
		18. Talk and listen
		19. Give it a go
		20. Keep on learning
Section objectives		• Recognise what role you can play in promoting change.
		• Be aware of techniques that can help you develop and evaluate your ideas for change.
		• Start to think about the role that children can play as leaders.

By now you will have some clear ideas about developing a culture of advocacy. We have thought about our own attitudes and ideas, and about how these play out in the different communities we are part of; we have thought about language and about the nature of opportunities. Step 5 allows you to focus on ways in which you might lead change within the settings that you share with children. Notably the idea of 'leadership' here is to be encouraged at every level as part of an evolving pattern of change that really can ensure positive transformation.

The previous chapters have offered many different ideas and steps that can be taken to bring about a culture of advocacy in which there is an ongoing focus on:

- establishing the child's voice: children's voices are acknowledged and valued

- amplifying the child's voice: opportunities are created that allow children's voices to be heard, giving others the chance to respond or engage.

What has been touched on throughout all of this is the role that you, as an adult, might play in bringing about a culture of advocacy. This chapter is about adults and children working together as partners. It is about identifying those first steps that can actually create real change!

So, where to begin…

DEFINING YOUR ROLE

Already the theme of power has been raised.

Adults have come in for some challenges in the previous pages of this book. This has meant the need to question our role as adults and our attitudes towards children. The point of this was not to de-value the adult but rather to increase the effectiveness of adults to draw out children's potential.

A common term used has been 'partner', although it is another 'p' that is often hovering in the background and which we must be aware of, and that is, of course, 'power'. Adults do have more power than children. It is a power that for a number of reasons will not just go away. However, that power that adults have does not need to be used in order to control children; rather it can be used to empower them, as adults facilitate opportunities which allow the voice of the child to be heard.

An active coach

There are lots of different terms used to describe the types of role that adults play in working alongside children. 'Facilitator', 'coach', 'mentor' might be three. Particular meanings have arisen around these words, which are interpreted through a variety of training courses and resources. The aim here is not to point to the differences, but, rather, draw out from these ideas approaches that might benefit you in leading a culture of advocacy.

A theme repeated throughout this book has been the extent to which a culture of advocacy provides children with the chance to develop their skills and further their potential. The role of the adult therefore becomes one of helping children to negotiate the barriers they might find in their way. This reflects the role of a coach.

Like many of the terms discussed in this book, 'coaching' has a lot of associated meanings. Many of us will connect coaching with sports. The problem is that for many of us, our experience of doing sport as a child was defined by adults giving us 'instruction' rather than 'coaching'.

The difference between coach and instructor was a defining aspect of the writings of Timothy Gallwey (1976, 1981), a US academic. He explored tennis, golf and skiing and argued that the barrier to achieving your best performance was not necessarily your competition (who you were up against) but yourself – what is in our own head. Coaching, therefore, is about us managing those internal barriers as the coach helps to structure a way of thinking that allows the individual to learn their way to maximising their potential.

It seems easy and logical to blend this idea of the coach with that of the 'facilitator'. A facilitator is a role that has application, for example, in the classroom. A facilitator stands in contrast to a traditional teaching role and the hierarchical sharing of information, as they focus on creating opportunities through which the individual can discover that information for themselves. Notably, research reflects the extent to which ideal learning communities are characterised by the role of adults as facilitators, supporting children as together (adult and child) they journey through a learning task (with an emphasis on the journey and not the destination). Well-known educationalist Ken Robinson talks about the role of the facilitator as one that is full of complexity and skill, and at its best it is nothing short of an 'art form' (Robinson 2015). We should therefore not underestimate our challenge as adults to carry out this role, for if we are to successfully develop a culture of advocacy we need to know how, when and in what ways to support the child in recognising the value in their voice and how it can be used.

It is, therefore, by bringing facilitating and coaching together – with the term 'active coaching' – that a role emerges that puts us as adults in a strong place to drive forward a culture of advocacy. 'Active coaching', therefore, is about recognising the importance of the role that adults can play in creating connections, which can have an impact on the individual and the way in which they think about themselves, through initiating opportunities that support this journey of self discovery.

To lead change an 'active coach' needs to:

- Action 17: Have an idea

- Action 18: Talk and listen

- Action 19: Give it a go

- Action 20: Keep on learning.

These steps combine those two themes for advocacy that we have been exploring:

1. establishing the voice of the child

2. amplifying that voice.

The table below sets out the core actions for Step 5 in the context of two possible stages for building a project. The first encourages you to engage with children's voices as you seek to shape the project. The second is about creating the most effective platform and opportunities that allow that voice to be heard.

17: Have an Idea		18: Talk & Listen		19: Give it a Go		20: Keep on Learning
Stage 1: Establish the voice of the child – shaping a project						
Your idea or their idea	➤	Is it the right idea (or an idea shaped by assumptions?)	➤	Test the idea out – do you need to speak to some/more children?	➤	Outcome: What have you found out and so what is next?
Stage 2: Amplifying children's voices – delivering a project						
Shape the opportunities you wish to offer	➤	Put your plan of action together	➤	Give the project a go	➤	Outcomes: What have you learnt? What have you achieved?
Ongoing: Review						
Image of the child		Motivation		Positioning of children's voices		
(see Step 2 for more detail)						

ACTION 17: HAVE AN IDEA: INTRODUCING CHANGE

Creating an effective culture of advocacy allows ideas to emerge from the bottom up – the leader as an 'active coach' facilitates that idea and allows it to grow.

In pretty much all of the spaces that we share with children there is an expectation that adults are the leaders, and within this certain adults in particular:

- In school, this might be the principal

- In the home, the parent

- and so on…

The result is that we often leave the task of having the ideas to those people. It is not part of our job description. Indeed, many organisations are created around a hierarchical structure that limits the opportunity for ideas to not only be heard but acted on. The challenge is heightened by the fact that those at the top of this pyramid often lack the time to be creative, to engage with the ideas, because they are so busy managing the day to day. So, we ask again, who is the leader?

As we saw in Step 1, how we think about children matters. The starting point in this book was for us to question and challenge our perception and our assumptions about children. A reinvigorated image of the child and the recognised connection to effective practice, and ultimately to children's experience, should form the foundation for our ideas. With this knowledge you, and increasingly over time, the children, become the leaders of change, the source for ideas!

An idea that establishes the voice of the child, as suggested in the introduction to this approach, is one that allows for them to make a call for action. It allows them to present a thought:

- School meals should taste better.

- Our play park should have different equipment.

- Our library should have this resource.

- My experience of the supermarket would be better if…

So what is your idea?

There are many different motivational lines about journeys. But the crux of all of them is that no journey can ever be completed unless it starts – with that first step.

While visiting a school I met a 6-year-old girl who had set up a club in school. 'My club is called "We can change the world"', she told me. Notwithstanding that the vision of the club was big, this young leader had taken that important first move – she had an idea. She understood that to start with this might mean trying to sit down with her two friends and asking them why they found it hard to always get on with one another. But she knew she had to start somewhere!

So, again, what is *your* idea?

Think! Find an (Newtonian) apple tree to stand under! Go for a walk! Listen to some music!

Once you have that eureka moment then say the idea out loud, write it down, text it to a friend – take that first step and breathe life into it.

ACTION 18: TALK AND LISTEN: CREATING CHANGE

Having the idea is a start; it is now time to bring it to life.

A key focus throughout this book has been the importance of bringing people together. To move from an idea to some defined steps for change, you are going to need to talk and listen to others as you move the idea from a personal thought to something that is 'shared'. This might mean (you or the children) talking to:

- *adults*: if we are to bring about change we may need to change adult attitudes (see Step 1). Conversations can be the starting point for exploring those attitudes as we engage others through actions suggested in Step 2.

- *children*: is the idea you have the right idea? Whether an adult or child has generated this idea – see what others think. Particularly when adults speak to children about an idea they might tell us that we have completely missed the point, helping us to shape the idea into something more relevant.

If you are developing any project that is going to benefit children and increase the scope of their advocacy, they need to be involved from the start. So get talking and most importantly don't forget to listen (Step 2 and Step 3 contain ideas for furthering conversations).

Talk and listen, therefore, is really about establishing the voice of the child. It is about exploring ideas and considering whether those ideas have relevance. It is about encouraging creativity and creating the right basis on which to build an effective project.

CASE STUDY

Think who you're talking to

I ran a university course in which students were asked to create their own advocacy project with children. As part of the build-up to this project I asked the group to experiment with some ideas. They were simply instructed to come up with an idea that could make university life better. They were given one hour to frame the idea and to present it to the class. At the end of the hour ideas were presented. In response I only had one question. 'How do you know?' The point of the exercise was to see whether they sought the views of others in presenting their 'good' idea. Whose voice were they representing?

In developing their advocacy project it was important that it was not their idea they were representing but rather an idea that had been explored as children's voices were engaged with and a 'shared idea' emerged.

Through talking and listening you should reach a point where you arrive at a shared idea. It is now time to give it a go!

ACTION 19: GIVE IT A GO

By talking and listening we can work towards children establishing their voice; now they need a platform from which that voice can be heard and, most importantly, responded to.

Step 4 offers some thinking that can help to create those platforms. They might range from developing some online resources, to children setting up meetings with key adults, to putting on an event to raise awareness. The project you develop will be unique to the 'call' that the children have presented.

However, as you think about a project do not let a fear of failure stop you from just giving it a go!

One of the big issues for us in schools is freeing children from their concerns over making a mistake and freeing them up to see mistakes as simply part of a journey. It is the same for us as adults.

You have an idea and you have consulted on it. It is an idea that will allow children's voices to be heard; the next step is to create a platform or set of opportunities that allows those voices to be amplified and to have an impact.

The table below (see Resource Sheet 8) offers some guidance steps for thinking about your project. Whatever the size of the idea, the steps can be useful in shaping a plan of action.

Throughout, keep reviewing your own assumptions and make sure that it is the voice of the child that is being given the chance to really be heard.

Your project action 19: Give it a go

Elements	Description	Example (from a student project)
Project name	You might wish to give your project a name.	Free to grow.
Your idea	What is the project all about?	Our goal is not to eradicate child prostitution but to raise awareness of the issue and educate individuals on the effects and risks associated with such lifestyles.
Objectives	Break your idea down into smaller objectives	Building coalitions Engaging with children Sharing our message.

cont.

Elements	Description	Example (from a student project)
Activities	consider some practical steps that you can take to make each of your objectives happen. It is important that these activities are: • Clear: Make each activity clear and definable • Realistic: Have you got the capacity to make this happen? What staff would you need? What would that mean in relation to funding? Will it fit within your timescales? • Measurable: how are you going to measure it. You can link this to the SMART criteria too: Specific Measurable Achivable Relevant Time-bound	Engaging with children (objective 2 from above. To gather children's voices and through this an understanding of the issues that children face… Create non threatening environments for children to speak out and to work with them to establish platforms that allow their voices to be heard. Engage with children's needs and desires.

ACTION 20: KEEP ON LEARNING: EVALUATING/MAINTAINING CHANGE

Reflecting on your outcomes is an important part of any project (again, whatever the size). In a continuation of the table above (see Resource Sheets 9 and 10), here are some criteria that you could use to measure your advocacy project. These offer a formal set of measures that might be of value in presenting the idea to an external group (such as funders), but they are also of use for simply making the most out of the experience.

Your project Action 20 Keep on learning	Elements	Description	Example (from a student project)
	Project name		Continually Review Motivation & image Continually review Motivation & image Continually review Motivation & image
	Your idea		
	Objectives		
	Activities		
	Targets/ Milestones	Define in a quantifiable way what the target is for each of your activities. This might be to set a figure for the number of children you intend to engage with. Note this will only have meaning if it is linked to a timescale.	*Activity:* To gather children's voices and through this an understanding of the issues that children face. *Target:* In the first three months of the project we will have gathered the views of 60 children.

cont.

Elements	Description	Example (from a student project)
Means of Assessment (to evaluate target)	Describe what means will you use to measure whether you have reached your target.	*Target*: In the first three months of the project we will have gathered the views of 60 children. *Means of assessment*: We will count the number of children's views gathered according to the number of interviews we have recorded and transcribed.
Evaluation criteria – measuring impact (Monitoring and evaluation systems)	How do you intend to evaluate impact? There are many different ways in which you can evaluate impact. Here are some examples of criteria that could be used to help measure impact on an advocacy project: • Do children have a growing awareness of their rights? • Are there any meaningful changes to policy and practice that encourage children's voices? • To what extent have perceptions about equity and non-discrimination changed? • Have the number and nature of opportunities for children's participation altered? • Has children's sense of themselves as citizens changed? • Is there an alteration within the wider community of the value of children's participation? (see also Save the Children, 2007: 16) You will need to design your own criteria through which you can measure impact.	*Objective*: Engage with children Example evaluation criteria: To see, through the sharing of children's authentic voice, a change in attitude amongst the local community. Children grow in awareness of their rights. Here, change is going to be defined by the change in adult attitudes, therefore this will be monitored by interviewing adults within the local community and seeing how they are engaging with our project. We will run a questionnaire with children at the start, at six months and at 12 months to see if their understanding of children's rights has changed.

Measuring children's participation	A key part of our projects is that we establish the voice of the child and then amplify it. It is going to be really helpful if we, therefore, have a key measure that is going to allow us to assess children's participation. This of course is linked to the change criteria above so you might wish to connect them – but it is important that you specifically address how children are going to be involved.	See table below (Resource Sheet 9) – this is a useful resource for helping you think carefully about children's involvement. The table helps you to question and justify to yourself why you might not want children to be involved. Also see tables from Step 4.
Updated targets	It is important that you give an indication of how you are going to respond if you do not meet the targets that you have set yourself. What is your plan B?	

Keep a record of the project:

A way of helping to shape our learning is to set targets or goals and to use these as points at which to review and reflect on what you have achieved. This can then form part of a journal or a professional development group or just a network of like-minded people (see the following section).

Dissemination:

If it works then why not share it. If you have managed to capture the project and have some measures of impact, then find a way to share that idea with others.

Action 20: Keep on learning

Children and young people's involvement in:	Level of child and youth participation			
	Not involved	Receive information and services	Provide input	Responsible for planning and action
Planning the service or project				
Recruiting staff				
Selecting leaders and volunteers				
Delivering the service				
Reviewing and evaluating the service				
Training and peer education				
Policy advocacy work				
Other:				
Other:				
Other:				

(Source – Save the Children, 2007: 67)

ONGOING REFLECTION

The steps above offer a more formal model for exploring outcomes linked to your project. However, the ongoing effectiveness of ideas comes from one's ability to continue to learn. The tools below offer practical ways in which you, with children, can reflect on what you are doing and seek to build on the positives and to use those to further amplify children's voices as you encourage leaders of change.

Action research

There are loads of different ways to keep on learning, including:

- reading books

- taking courses

- talking with others.

However, one that we have found particularly relevant in the context of working with children is action research.

Action research, in this context, is merely a way in which you as an individual or as a group can review what you are doing in order to make it a focus of attention and conversation, and through this make your practice better.

Here is an overview of how you might incorporate action research into your culture of advocacy as a tool for reflection (for more on action research, see Frankel and Fowler 2016):

1. Find a starting point.

2. Review your practice.

3. Identify the positives.

4. Identify the challenges.

5. Identify the mountain peaks and pitfalls.

Finding a starting point

Have a think about what you are doing. What aspect of it would you like to understand more? Often when we search for a starting point, we head to an aspect of the project that is not working. However, how about finding an aspect of the project that works well but that could be made outstanding?

Sometimes in creating a starting point it is important to be objective. Think about an aspect of the project that is going to really have a wider impact on furthering children's voices.

An example for a starting point might be: How can children be encouraged to be more independent in sharing their voice?

Note: For action research to work – you need some 'practice' to focus in on. So pick something you are already doing or link it to a new activity you are undertaking.

Review your practice

The cycle of a project has been identified above, from having an idea, talking and listening, to giving it a go and evaluating it. Action research sits alongside this process. Use your starting point or question from above to give you the focus for collecting examples of this in action. By creating a focus for attention you will start to see things you had not seen before.

Take photos, videos, keep a journal, keep activities that you do (for example, any pictures, worksheets, flipchart activities). This does not need to be time consuming – just keep it simple.

What you have collected now becomes a focus for your own thoughts and ideas and, of course, conversations with others.

The positives

From what you have collected, identify some positives. What worked well? Share these with others, showing them your evidence and sharing your experience.

A great way of encouraging individuals or a team to reflect on the positives is to ask them about the impact they have had using this ripple model (see Resource Sheet 11):

Describe any impact in the wider community:

Describe the impact within your setting:

Describe the impact on you (adults):

Describe the impact on children:

What action is your focus?

The challenges
What does the data you have collected show in terms of 'challenges'? What did you find as you took the journey? Where were you not so effective?

The mountain peaks and pitfalls
What is to be aimed towards or avoided as this project develops (or can you see application in other areas)?

Note: The benefit comes from collecting the examples and from sharing and discussing this with others.

Reflect on these in light of Steps 1, 2, 3 and 4. This is a simplified model for introducing action research.

ACTIVE COACHING WITH CHILDREN
Action research encourages the individual to reflect on the process; what active coaching does is it allows children to increasingly direct the journey for themselves. Leadership within a culture of advocacy is about recognising one's own value and being able to do something with it. The following approach, which we are increasingly exploring in schools,

allows children to engage with Actions 17, 18, 19 and 20 in such a way that it allows them to build up a sense of value in themselves and what they can achieve – so that they can increasingly lead a culture of advocacy.

Have an idea

It should not be a surprise that classical mathematician Archimedes (as the legend would have us believe) was so delighted on coming up with an idea that he shouted 'Eureka!' (You might have cried that too – on coming up with your 'ideas' earlier in Step 5. However, as you know it can be a challenge to get to that point.)

Active coaching with children starts by identifying what it is that one might work towards; what goal or personal objective could be the focus. The point is that the process encourages us to be more effective in vocalising our ideas.

A: What is the issue (what do you want to change)?
COACH:

Ask: Have you identified any issues or challenges (offer a context)? Have you any ideas of what you could change?

Support questions may include:

- What do you want to achieve?

- What do you feel you are good at? What do you feel you are not so good at?

- What areas of your life do you feel confident and sure about? What areas do you feel muddled and confused about?

- In which areas of your life do you think you could create positive change?

COACHEE:
The emphasis here is on the coachee. The questions asked by the coach may encourage the thinking, but ideally you are aiming for a point at which the coachee has the idea and then turns to the coach for support.

Initially the 'ideas' around issues, challenges and change could be quite general; for example, 'I want to be more confident'. As the process moves on this will become increasingly more refined.

Talk and listen

B: Why is it an issue? Why is the change needed?
COACH:
A key part of this strategy is the 'coach' drawing out the details of the issue, so that this can become something defined and the 'coachee' can then identify some strategies to manage it. Here are some questions that might help in narrowing down on what exactly the issue is...

Ask: What is the current situation?

Tell me about why you have chosen...?

Invite the coachee to view the issue from different perspectives. 'Imagine you are hovering in a helicopter, what do you see?'

C: Spotting the obstacles

Ask:

- Why do you think this is an issue/needs change?
- How does it make you feel?
- What are you missing/don't you have?
- Does the setting you are in or the people you are with have an impact? Why? How?

Once you have an idea of what the issue is you can then think about finding a solution.

D. Identifying solutions

Ask:

- What ideas do you have that might help you to deal with this issue?

- What could you actually change?

- What might that personal change look like?

- How might you bring that change about? What steps do you need to take?

It helps to have a set of example solutions that children can engage with as they explore what might work.

Coachee:
Throughout, it is important that the coachee is able to focus in on:

- a specific personal issue that can be addressed (the focus here is on what steps the coachee can personally take to bring about change)

- a clear sense of what the obstacles are (again being realistic)

- making use of the 'coach' as a sounding board to identify solutions

- identifying a realistic and achievable 'solution' to have a go at.

Give it a go!

E. Giving your solution a go
COACHEE:

The coachee needs to try and put their solution into practice. For this to be really effective, they need to commit to giving that solution a proper try with both their head and heart. They need to believe that it is manageable and they need to feel that they want to see a change.

Keep on learning

Even after you have had an idea, refined this using talking and listening, and come up with an approach or solution, the process does not end. Rather, it is key that you find the time to reflect and re-assess how things have gone and are continuing to go. As such it offers the opportunity to explore how an idea or solution might have wider application.

F: Making use of a solution or finding a new one
COACH:

Ask:

- How effective were your solutions?

- Why do you think they worked or did not work? (If they did not work – return to B)

- How and where might you be able to continue to use what you have learnt?

As you reflect on the process (use the headings from action research to help).

COACHEE:

They need to try and think about what worked and how this could be applied somewhere else! Look for other places where you can put these solutions into practice. Then, have a new 'idea' and start the process again.

Note: this is a simplified version of a far more developed model that is emerging within our work in schools. If you would like to explore this further, do get in touch.

This model can be used with individuals or groups. It can be used by adults working with children, the other way round or by children working with other children.

CONCLUSION

In presenting a culture of advocacy, the aim has been to introduce a reflective process that reminds us, as adults, of the value of children's voices.

As society has learnt, it is only by recognising the individual, whatever their gender or skin colour or indeed age, that members of a community can truly grow together. Step 1 highlighted what we can learn from history and the need to look beyond assumptions that have fuelled resistance to the contribution of some individuals. By challenging our own attitudes we can sift out those views that get in the way of us opening the door to children's participation.

In essence Step 1 was an invitation for us to remember to keep re-tuning our antenna to the positive 'noise' that reflects children's active role in the world around them, as we shrug off those assumptions that have for too long dominated adult engagement with children.

As part of the detox process, we also need to recognise that the settings that we share with children can also be tainted by assumptions as we create an approach shaped by images of the child and particular motivations for engaging with them. Step 2 was about starting a conversation, therefore, which explores any rhetoric/reality gap as we look at children's place and purpose in these common spaces. What has consistently emerged as part of our work in schools is a separation between adult assessments of the space and the experience of children.

To narrow that gap, a conversation is essential; however, we must not get complacent, it is important to remember that no matter where we are on our journey, we need to keep 'talking'.

Step 3 offered some specific 'ingredients' that could be used as part of establishing a culture of advocacy within a setting. From identifying 'characteristics' around the child as advocate, through to considering a vocabulary around participation, research and emotions, the relevance of a shared language was introduced. Notably, this was not about creating a universal language, but rather about encouraging you to think about a language that is relevant to you and others within your setting and which would allow effective engagement from children and adults alike. Step 3 reiterated the need for asking questions as we, as adults, continue to develop our knowledge and understanding about the children we engage with (perhaps by inviting children to help build up that knowledge through their own research).

Making the most of an opportunity was the intention behind Step 4. It offered some headings to help think about the nature of the opportunities we create, so that they can provide chances for children to not only grow in confidence about the value of their voice but also to construct those platforms that will allow them to amplify that voice. The actions in this step, therefore become a springboard from which you and the children you work with can innovate as you seek to shape opportunities that are going to have the right impact in the context of the ideas that you are exploring. Step 4 reminded us that opportunities do not need to be about creating worldwide change, but are as much about the role children can play in small community-based changes, for example at home or school.

Change is needed. That change might need to start with you. Step 5 sought to encourage you to give it a go. Change is never neat and it will never fit into boxes on resource sheets in a book; however, the tools within this step do provide a framework to guide your efforts, and those of the children you live or work with, to create a 'culture of advocacy'. A culture in which children's voices are acknowledged and valued and where opportunities are constantly being created that allows children's voices to be heard and from which others are given the chance to respond or engage with what they hear.

A closing call to action: A May Day rally in 2017 in the Czech city of Brno would not necessarily be the place to look for an international news story. However, as Neo-Nazis marched through the streets, a small group of scouts, in their uniforms, stood proudly with home-drawn banners. One of the group was 16-year-old Lucie Myslíková. Lucie and her friends had chosen to offer an alternative view to that of the marching group. They had a voice which they felt should be heard. Even when Lucie was confronted by one of the Neo-Nazis she stood her ground and continued to represent her ideas. It was this image of a calm but determined Lucie facing the more vociferous, short-haired, black-clothed, white male that resonated around the world.

We, as a society, should want all our children to have that confidence to 'establish' their voice and to then find the opportunities through which their voice can be 'amplified'. As we hear more from children and engage with their voices and their ideas, communities will change for the better. Simply our ability to protect and provide for the child will become increasingly accurate and more effective. A culture of advocacy invites us to recognise the value of children's voices in all those spaces that we share with them, as we as adults move from being the problem to being part of the solution. A culture of advocacy gives the communities within which we live and work the chance to find a 'common good' or shared agenda, as, by encouraging the voice of the individual child, adults grow to recognise and value children's place and purpose as active members of society.

RESOURCE SHEETS

1. Thinking about children

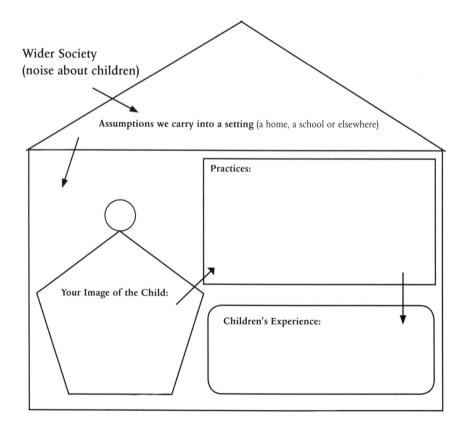

**Wider Society
(noise about children)**

Assumptions we carry into a setting (a home, a school or elsewhere)

Practices:

Your Image of the Child:

Children's Experience:

2. Action 8: Applying an Image

List of images	Description	Amount reflected in setting	Conclusion (assessment of image in that setting)
Object	Simply a specimen to be observed		
Subject	Acknowledge the particular nature of the child and the importance of engaging with it – although this remains adult directed		
Social Agent	Recognition of children potential as competent and active participants (but without creating opportunities for this to be put into practice)		
Co-participant	Not only acknowledge children as social agents above but also actively create opportunities for their participation including change making activities with adults		

3. Action 10: How you see children

Element of focus	Assessment of motivation	Assessment of image What are you trying to say? What are you trying to do? How are children's voices represented?	Recommendations
Website/ Written Materials	Mission/ Vision		
	Organisational Aims		
	Description of Projects/ Activities		
	Annual Review		
	Newsletter		

4. Action 10: How you see children

Focus	(Circle or add in your question) How do you see children? How do you see adults? Where do you hear children's voices? Your question:
Notes of Conversation	

Analysis	Assessment of Motivation	Assessment of Image	Recommendations
		Language	
		Activities to establish voice of child	
		Representation of voice	

5. Methods guidance

Method	Description	Advantages	Disadvantages
Interviews	Ask another person questions. *Your role* to decide what type of interview and what questions to ask.	Great to explore people's feelings Investigate ideas in detail Can ask lots of open questions	Leading questions or closed questions might limit the information you get. You will need to make a record of your interview this can take time. You need to practice your interviewing techniques.
	A helpful note: There are 3 types of interview: Structured – you have a clear plan, Semi-structured – you have a bit of a plan, Unstructured – no plan		
Focus Groups	Ask a group of about 5 people to explore the issues. *Your role* to guide the conversation, for this you will need to prepare some questions.	It can be a great way to include people. You can get different people's opinions.	You will need to practice your focus group skills. The group can lose direction. Your role is just to support the conversation not to direct it.
Observation	Watch what is going on and make notes. *Your role* to think about what you want to be looking out for. Then to watch but not interfere.	It can allow you to ask lots of people. It gives you data you can turn into numbers that you can use to help you present your findings.	You can't go into too much detail. The design of the questionnaire is important. You will need to think very carefully about the type of questions that you ask.
	A helpful note: A questionnaire might allow you to support your research through putting your findings into numbers - 10 out of 100 think this – it can be a useful means for sharing your findings.		
Creative/Action based methods	Photographs Videos Drawing Maps Drama	A range of ideas that are really good for getting people involved and investigating the issues in a slightly different way. If you want to use one of these techniques, find out more and give it a go!	

6. Actions 13, 14, 15 and 16: Assessing opportunities 1

What is the setting?
Who is going to be involved in this opportunity?
What characteristics/attributes would you like children to experience as part of this opportunity?
What is this opportunity?

This opportunity/ platform	How is this visible?	How might this be added to?	Your action steps
Encourages the individual			
Creates relevant experiences			
Empowers children as change makers			
Is **Ambitious** in scope and intended outcomes			

7. Action 13: Assessing opportunities 2

Opportunity to be assessed (from example – school council meetings)			
	How encouraged	How displayed	Recommendations
Self confidence (willingness to share ideas)			
Self respect (sense of purpose – you are meant to be there)			
Self esteem (sense of value – you can make a particular contribution)			

8. Action 19: Give it a go

Elements	Description	Example (from a student project)
Project name	You might wish to give your project a name.	
Your idea	What is the project all about?	
Objectives	Break your idea down into smaller objectives	
Activities	Consider some practical steps that you can take to make each of your objectives happen. It is important that these activities are: **Clear**: Make each activity clear and definable **Realistic**: Have you got the capacity to make this happen? What staff would you need? What would that mean in relation to funding? Will it fit within your timescales? **Measurable**: How are you going to measure it. You can link this to the SMART criteria too: **Specific** **Measurable** **Achivable** **Relevant** **Time-bound**	

9. Reviewing your project

Elements	Description	Example (from a student project)
Targets/ Milestones		
Means of Assessment (to evaluate target)		
Evaluation criteria – measuring impact (Monitoring and evaluation systems)		
Measuring children's participation	Link to resource	
Updated targets		
Ongoing Review of Motivation and Image		

10. Action 20: Keep on learning

Children and young people's involvement in:	Level of child and youth participation			
	Not involved	Receive information and services	Provide input	Responsible for planning and action
Planning the service or project				
Recruiting staff				
Selecting leaders and volunteers				
Delivering the service				
Reviewing and evaluating the service				
Training and peer education				
Policy advocacy work				
Other:				
Other:				
Other:				

11. The Impact Ripple Effect

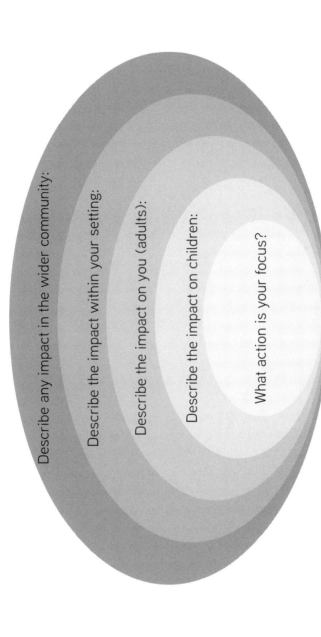

Describe any impact in the wider community:

Describe the impact within your setting:

Describe the impact on you (adults):

Describe the impact on children:

What action is your focus?

USEFUL RESOURCES

General
Frankel, S. and Fowler, J. (2016) *How to Take Your School on a Journey to Outstanding.* Church Stretton: EquippingKids.

Academic
Cockburn, T. (2013) *Rethinking Children's Citizenship.* Basingstoke: Palgrave Macmillan.

Percy-Smith, B. and Thomas, N. (2010) *A Handbook of Children and Young People's Participation: Perspectives from Theory and Practice.* New York/London: Routledge.

Frankel, S. (2017) *Negotiating Childhoods.* Basingstoke: Palgrave Macmillan.

Tisdall, K., Gadda, A. and Butler, U. (eds) (2014) *Children and Young People's Participation and its Transformative Potential.* Basingstoke: Palgrave Macmillan.

Getting started
McNamee, S. (2016) *The Social Study of Childhood.* Basingstoke: Palgrave Macmillan.

Steps 1 and 2
Bluebond-Langner, M. (1978) *The Private World of Dying Children.* Princeton, NJ: Princeton University Press.

Cunningham, H. (2006) *The Invention of Childhood,* London: BBC.

Gatto, J.T. (2005) *Dumbing Us Down: The Hidden Curriculum of Compulsory Schooling.* Gabriola Island: New Society Publishers, Gabriola Island.

Kohn, A. (2005) *Unconditional Parenting.* New York: Atria Books.

UNICEF Child Friendly Cities: www.childfriendlycities.org

Martha Payne's food Blog: www.neverseconds.blogspot.co.uk

Challenging attitudes towards gender: www.plan-international.org

International ages of criminal responsibility: www.crin.org/en/home/ages

Step 3

RIGHTS

Alderson, P. (2008) *Young Children's Rights.* London: Jessica Kingsley Publishers.
Jans, J. (2004) 'Children as citizens: Towards a contemporary notion of child participation.' *Childhood 11*, 1, 27–44.
www.unicef.org.uk/what-we-do/un-convention-child-rights

PARTICIPATION

Hart, R. (1992) *Children's Participation: From Tokenism to Citizenship.* Florence: UNICEF International Child Development Centre.
Shier, H. (2001) 'Pathways to participation: Openings, opportunities and obligations.' *Children and Society 15*, 107–117.

RESEARCH

Bucknall, S. (2012) *Children as Researchers in Primary Schools.* London: Routledge.
Cesesma (2012) 'Learn to Live without Violence: Transformative research by children and young people.' Matagalpa, Nicaragua and Preston, UK: Cesesma and the Centre for Children and Young People's Participation.

Step 4

O'Neill, K. (2007) 'Getting It Right for Children: A Practitioners' Guide to Child Rights Programming. Save the Children.' Retrieved March 21, 2017 from   https://resourcecentre.savethechildren.net/library/getting-it-right-children-practitioners-guide-child-rights-programming
PRA principles | Participatory Methods. (n.d.) from Institute of Development Studies. Retrieved June 27, 2017 from www.participatorymethods.org/subjects/pra-principles
UNICEF Child Friendly Cities: www.childfriendlycities.org
Innovative efforts towards engagement: www.hole-in-the-wall.com/Beginnings.html
Children's radio project: www.childrencount.org.za/radio/index.php

Step 5

Covey, S.R. (2008) *The Leader in Me: How Schools and Parents around the World Are Inspiring Greatness, One Child at a Time.* New York: Free Press.
Save the Children (2006) *Children and Young People as Citizens: Partners for Social Change.* Kathmandu, Nepal: Save the Children Sweden.
Whitmore, J. (2009) *Coaching for Performance: Growing Human Potential and Purpose.* London: Nicholas Brealey Publishing.
Wright, A. and Jaffe, K. (2014) *Six Steps to Successful Child Advocacy: Changing the World for Children.* London: Sage.

Note: Many of the ideas in this book represent a changing way of thinking and your engagement will add to that. We would very much like to hear more about your journey and whether there is any way we can support it, so do 'join the conversation' at www.equippingkids.org

BIBLIOGRAPHY

Abc7 (24/4/2017) 'Former president Obama speaks at University of Chicago'. Retrieved 3rd October 2017 from http://abc7chicago.com/news/former-president-obama-speaks-at-u-of-c/1910280.

Alderson, P. (1995) *Listening to Children: Children, Ethics and Social Research*. Ilford: Barnardos.

All Party Parliamentary Group for Children (APPGC) (2014) 'It's all about trust.' Building good relationships between children and the police.' London: APPGC and NCB.

Butler, V. (2012) 'An Explanation of How Ethics Inform the Design of Social Research with Children Under 11 Years of Age.' In E. Fleming and T. Boeck (eds) *Involving Children and Young People in Health and Social Care Research*. London: Routledge.

Bacon, K. and Frankel, S. (2014) 'Rethinking children's citizenship: Negotiating structure, shaping meanings.' *International Journal of Children's Rights 22*, 1, 21–43.

BBC (2015) 'Rotherham abuse victims tell their stories.' *BBC News,* 5 February. Retrieved 27 June 2017 from www.bbc.co.uk/news/uk-england-south-yorkshire-28971058.

Brooks, L. (2003) 'Kid power.' *Guardian Weekend,* 26 April.

CALMzine (2017) 'Exclusive: William and Harry in their own words', *Calmzine,* 25 April. Retrieved 21 September 2017 from www.thecalmzone.net/2017/04/exclusive-william-harry-words.

Casey, L. (2015) 'Report of an inspection of Rotherham Metropolitan Borough Council.' HM Government: Department for Communities and Local Government.

Chambers, R. (1983) *Rural Development: Putting the Last First*. Harlow: Prentice Hall.

Cockburn, T. (2013) *Rethinking Children's Citizenship*. Basingstoke: Palgrave Macmillan.

Cunningham, S. and Lavalette, M. (2004) '"Active citizens" or "Irresponsible truants"? School student strikes against the war.' *Critical Social Policy 24*, 2, 255–269.

Dobash, R.E. and Dobash, R.P. (1979) *Violence Against Wives*. New York: Free Press.

Dobash, R.E. and Dobash, R. (1992) *Women, Violence, and Social Change*. New York/London: Routledge.

Donaldson, M. and McGarrigle, J. (1975) 'Conversation accidents.' *Cognition 3*, 34, 1–50.

Equiano, O. (1789) *Sold as a Slave*. Penguin: London.

Frankel, S. (2012) *Children, Morality and Society*. Basingstoke: Palgrave Macmillan.

Frankel, S. (2015) 'Researching Social Agency and Morality: Theory and Practice for Working with Younger Children.' In O. Saracho (ed.) *Handbook of Research Methods in Early Childhood Education: Review of Research Methodologies Volume 11*. Charlotte, NC: Information Age Publishing.

Frankel, S. (2017) *Negotiating Childhoods*. Basingstoke: Palgrave Macmillan.

Frankel, S., McNamee, S. and Pomfret, A. (2015) 'Approaches to promoting ideas about children's rights and participation: Can the education of undergraduate students contribute to raising the visibility of the child in relation to child participation in Canada?' *Canadian Journal of Children's Rights*.

Frankel, S. and Fowler, J. (2016) *How to Take Your School on a Journey to Outstanding*. Church Stretton: EquippingKids.

Gallwey, W.T. (1976) *Inner Tennis: Playing the Game*, 1st edition. New York: Random House.

Gallwey, W.T. (1981) *The Inner Game of Golf*. New York: Random House.

Gillick v West Norfolk and Wisbech Health Authority and Another. 1986 1 FLR 250.

Hart, R. (1992) *Children's Participation: From Tokenism to Citizenship*. Florence: UNICEF International Child Development Centre.

Hart, R. and Schwab, M. (1997) 'Children's rights and the building of democracy: A dialogue on the international movement for children's participation.' *Social Justice 24*, 3.

Honneth, A. (1995) *The Struggle for Recognition: The Moral Grammar of Social Conflicts*. Cambridge: Polity Press.

James, A. and James, A.L. (2004) *Constructing Childhood*. Basingstoke: Palgrave Macmillan.

Kohn, A. (2005) *Unconditional Parenting*. New York: Attria Books.

Lansdown, G. (2010) 'The Realisation of Children's Participation Rights.' In B. Percy-Smith and N. Thomas (eds) *A Handbook of Children and Young People's Participation: Perspectives from Theory and Practice*. New York/London: Routledge.

Lewars, J. (2010) 'Nil Desperandum as long as You Carpe Drum.' In B. Percy-Smith and N. Thomas (eds) *A Handbook of Children and Young People's Participation: Perspectives from Theory and Practice*. New York/London: Routledge.

Lundy, L. (2007) '"Voice is not enough": Conceptualising Article 12 of the United Nations Convention on the Rights of the Child.' *British Educational Research Journal 33*, 6, 927–942.

Mayo, M. and Rooke, A. (2008) 'Active learning for active citizenship: Participatory approaches to evaluating a programme to promote citizen participation in England.' *Community Development Journal 43*,3, 371–381.

Meintjes, H. (2014) 'Growing up in Time of AIDS: The Shinning Recorders of Zisize.' In K. Tisdall, A. Gadda and U. Butler (eds) *Children and Young People's Participation and its Transformative Potential*. Basingstoke: Palgrave Macmillan.

Mortimer, J. (1998) *Clinging to the Wreckage*. London: Penguin.

O'Neill, K. (2007) Getting It Right for Children: A Practitioners' Guide to Child Rights Programming. Save the Children. Retrieved 21 March 2017 from https://resourcecentre.savethechildren.net/library/getting-it-right-children-practitioners-guide-child-rights-programming.

Piaget, J. (1975 [1935]) *The Moral Judgement of the Child*. London: Routledge and Kegan Paul.

Paine, T. (1791) *The Rights of Man. For the Use and Benefit of all Mankind. By Thomas Paine, Member of the French Convention; Late a Prisoner in the Luxembourg at Paris; Secretary to Congress during the American War and Author of Common Sense, &c. &c.* London: Printed and sold by Citizen Daniel Isaac Eaton, printer and bookseller to the Supreme Majesty of the people, at the Cock and Swine, No. 74, Newgate-street.

Roberts-Holmes, G. (2005) *Doing Your Early Years Research Project*. London: Paul Chapman Publishing.

Robinson, K. (2015) *Creative Schools*. London: Penguin.

Sarason, S.B. (1971) *The Culture of the School and the Problem of Change*. Boston, MA: Allen and Bacon.

Save the Children (2007) *Getting It Right for Children – A Practitioner's Guide to Child Rights Programming*. Retrieved on 21 September 2017 from www.resourcecentre.savethechildren.net/library/getting-it-right-children-practitioners-guide-child-rights-programming.

Savyasaachi, Butler, U.-M. (2014) 'Decolonizing the Notion of Participation of Children and Young People.' In K. Tisdall, A. Gadda and U. Butler (eds) *Children and Young People's Participation and its Transformative Potential*. Basingstoke: Palgrave Macmillan.

Shier, H. (2001) 'Pathways to Participation: Openings, opportunities and obligations', *Children and Society 15*, 107–117.

Scraton, P. (1997) 'Whose Childhood? What Crisis.' In P. Scraton (ed.) *Childhood in Crisis*. London: UCL Press.

UNESCO (2016) *Education for People and Planet: Creating Sustainable Futures for All*. Paris: UNESCO.

Urinboyev, R., Wickenberg, P. and Leo, U. (2016) 'Child rights, classroom and school management: A systematic literature review.' *The International Journal of Children's Rights 24*, 3, 522–547.

White, S. (1996) 'Depoliticising Development: The Uses and Abuses of Participation.' *Development in Practice 6*, 1, 6–15.

Wollstonecraft, M. (1792) *A Vindication of the Rights of Woman*. London: Penguin.

INDEX

A Vindication of the Rights of Women
   (Wollstonecraft) 37
aboriginal children
   60s scoop 77–8
   emotions and language 110–12
   government policies 41
action research 153–5
Active Citizens 95
active coaching 141–3, 155–60
Adams, John 34
adult-centrism 40–1
adults
   challenge to 25–6
   control 39–40
   as qualified 41
   as rescuers 40–1
   role and importance 14
advertising 80–1
advocacy, defining 15–17
advocacy model 20
age of criminal responsibility 31–3
aims and objectives
   getting started 11
   language 85
   leadership 139
   opportunity creation 114
   revitalising thinking 25
   spatial awareness 55
Alabed, Bana 16, 122–3
Alderson, P. 104
ambition, opportunity creation
   128–30, 134, 138

analysis and interpretation 108
APPGC 88
assumptions 29ff
   competence 35–9
   disability 129–30
   future child 35–9
   protected child 39–42
   universal child 30–5
Australia, aboriginal children 41

Bacon, K. 51
being, and becoming 51
Best Interests Doctrine 40, 79
Bird, W. 136
book
   aims 11, 13, 16, 161
   focus on voice 87
   questioning 14
   scope 13
bottom up/top down approaches
   137–8
Brazil, language 93
Brno rally 163
Brooks, L. 116
Butler, V. 92, 104, 105

call and response 16
CALMzine 26
'Campaign for a Commercial Free
   Childhood' 81

Canada
  60s scoop 77–8
  aboriginal children 41
  Child Advocacy Offices 65–6
  divorce and custody 79
  restorative justice 89
case studies
  60s scoop 77–8
  advertising 80–1
  asking questions 106
  bottom up/top down approaches
      125
  Child Advocacy Offices 65–6
  child-friendliness 57–8
  children in legal system 31–3
  children's voices 52–3
  community empowerment 135–8
  dental health 90–1
  disability 129–30
  divorce and custody 78–80
  emotions and language 110–12
  fairness 48–9
  Getting it Right for Children: A
      practitioner's guide to child
      rights programming 96
  Hapley School 87–8
  image of the child 44–5
  Iraq war school strikes 116–17
  museums 101–2
  online spaces 122
  parenting 131–4
  police and children 88–9
  power relations 127–8
  restaurants 76–7
  restorative justice 89–90
  Rotherham abuse case 58–9
  school council 69–70
  talking about emotions 112
  talking and listening 146
  teachers' attitudes 68
Casey, L. 58
Cesesma 98, 109
Chambers, R. 124
change
  creating 145–6

  evaluating and maintaining
      148–52
  thinking about 130
Child Advocacy Offices 65–6
Child Friendly Cities project 51
Childhood Studies 19
children
  active coaching 155–60
  and crime 43–4
  experience 47–9
  image of 42–5
  as passive/active 18–19
  perceptions of 17–19
  and police 88–9
  position of 14
  as researchers 108–9
  as unqualified 41
citizenship 51
citizenship classes 116–17
climate for change 23–4
co-operation, in research 107–8
co-participant, child as 64
coaching, active 141–3, 155–60
Cockburn, Tom 120
communication, questions 105–7
competence 35–9
confidence 163
consent 104
contested concepts 15
control, locus of 39–40
courts, universal child to individual
      child 50
crime, and children 43–4
culture of advocacy
  defining 56, 86, 115
  effectiveness 114–15
  effects of 17, 163
  elements 11–12
Cunningham, S. 116, 117

democracy 121
dental health 90–1
detox 27ff
developmental perspectives 40–1
developmental theories 35
difference, imagining 53–4

divorce
    children's voices 52–3
    and custody 78–80
Dobash, R.E. 38
Dobash, R.P. 38
domestic violence 38
Donaldson, M. 106

Eckert, Madison 125
Education2030 goals 95
emotions
    and language 109–13
    talking about 112
    as water patterns 111
empowering
    communities 135–8
    opportunity creation 123–8, 134,
        137–8
encouragement 132–3, 135–6
Equiano, Olaudah 36–7
EquippingKids 19
ethics 103–5
experience, children 47–9
exploitation 61

facilitators 141–2
fairness 48–9
fake news 29–30
focus groups 71–5
Fowler, John 19, 87, 110–12, 153
Frankel, Sam 17–19, 49, 51, 63, 87,
    102, 153
Freire, Paulo 124
'from hoodies to goodies' (Guardian)
    44
future child 35–9
    to active child 51

Gallwey, Timothy 141
Getting it Right for Children: A
    practitioner's guide to child
    rights programming (Save the
    Children) 96
getting started
    advocacy model 20

approach taken 19–21
approaching advocacy 13–15
defining advocacy 15–17
defining children 17–19
introducing advocacy 12–13
overview 11–12
steps 20–1
Gillick v West Norfolk HA 50
giving it a go 146–8, 159
    resource sheet 171
government policies, aboriginal
    children 41
Guardian 44
Gustoso 57–8

Hapley School 87–8
Harry 47–8
Hart, Roger 96–8
Hart's model 96–8
hierarchical model 14
Hindi 92
HIV 135–8
Honneth, A. 118–19

ideas
    and active coaching 156–7
    and leadership 143–5
identity, development 118–20
image and practice 45–7
    practice of others 46–8
image of the child 42–5
    refreshing 49–53
    resource sheets 164–7
imagining difference 53–4
impact ripple effect 154–5, 174
individuality, recognising 50
informal platforms, opportunity
    creation 121–3, 136–7
instrumental participation 126
internet 44
introducing advocacy, effects of
    12–13
Iraq war school strikes 116–17
issues, identifying 156–7

James, A. 62
James, A.L. 62
Josh and Nathan 48–9

King, Martin Luther Jr 15
Kohn, A. 45
Kuchyt, Sarah 89

language
  and advocacy 13–14
  application 95
  Brazil 93
  clarity 85–6
  conclusions 113
  consent 104
  and emotions 109–13
  ethics 103–5
  Hart's model 96–8
  Hindi 92
  and opportunity creation 123
  overview 85–6
  of participation 96–100
  questions 105–7
  reflections and conclusions 162
  research techniques 100–9
  of rights 93–6
  setting characteristics 86–91
  Shier's model 98–100
  South Africa 92–3
  speaking and listening 101
  talking about emotions 112
  see also technical vocabulary
language and tone 67
Lansdown, G. 33
Lavalette, M. 116, 117
lawyers, as advocates 13–14
leadership
  action research 153–5
  active coaching 141–3, 155–60
  creating change 145–6
  evaluating and maintaining change
    148–52
  giving it a go 146–8, 159
  ideas 143–5, 156–7
  identifying obstacles 157–8

identifying solutions 158
learning 148–52, 159
ongoing reflection 153–5
overview 139–40
power relations 140–3
reflections and conclusions 162–3
role definition 140–3
talking and listening 157
using solutions 159
learners, defining 19
learning
  leadership 148–52, 159
  resource sheet 173
  scope of 19–20
learning opportunities 86–7
legal system 31–3
'Let's save Africa' (video) 44–5
Lewars, J. 69–70
Lindsay 77–8
listening 101
  creating change 145–6
  opportunity creation 133–4
Locke, John 34
Lundy, L. 95

Mandela, Nelson 15
May Day rally, Brno 163
Mayo, M. 120
McGarrigle, J. 106
McNamee, S. 63
Meintjes, H. 136, 138
Mill, John Stuart 121
minority status, and competence
    36–9
Mortimer, Sir John 13–14
motivation
  activities and practices 67–8
  image of the child 63–6
  language and tone 67
  and view of children 60–1
multi-disciplinary approach 17–19
Myslíková, Lucie 163

Nadine 76–7
Nathan and Josh 48–9

Nicaragua, children as researchers 109
noise
    and image of the child 43–4, 164
    and internet 44
    and positive image 49–53
    recognising 27–9, 30
    tuning to 161
nominal participation 126

Obama, Barack 15, 23
object, child as 64
Obomsawin, Alanis 78
obstacles, identifying 157–8
online spaces, opportunity creation 122–3
Ontario
    Child Advocacy Offices 66
    divorce and custody 79
opportunity creation 14
    ambition 128–30, 134, 138
    assessment 118
    bottom up/top down approaches 124–8, 137–8
    community empowerment 135–8
    conclusions 130–1
    effective 117
    empowering 123–8, 134, 137–8
    encouragement 132–3, 135–6
    encouraging individuals 118–20
    informal platforms 121–3, 136–7
    and language 123
    listening 133–4
    online spaces 122–3
    overview 114–17
    parenting 131–4
    reflections and conclusions 162
    relevance 120–3
    resource sheets 169–70

Paine, Thomas 34
parenting 131–4
participation
    bottom up/top down approaches 124–8

and children's rights 62–3
    defining 92–3
    importance of 41
    language of 96–100
    types of 126–7
    and view of children 61
Participatory Rural Appraisal (PRA) 127
partnership, in research 107–8
personal ethos 54
philosophy, and the individual 34–5
Piaget, Jean 35, 106
platforms, for voices 16
police, and children 88–9
Pomfret, A. 63
positives, identifying 154–5
power relations
    and empowerment 127–8
    and fairness 48–9
    and leadership 140–3
practice
    reviewing 154
    setting characteristics 86–91
    and view of children 67–8
practice of others 46–8
profit, and view of children 61
project review, resource sheet 172
protected child 39–42
    to participating child 52
protection, and view of children 61
provision, and view of children 61
pupil parliament 12

Quebec, Child Advocacy Offices 66
questions 105–7, 108

Rahfaldt, M. 136
reflections
    ambition 130
    and conclusions 161–3
    detox 29
    effects of practice 49
    getting started 21
    image and practice 46
    image of the child 45

reflections *cont.*
  language 91
  language models 100
  noise and image 53
  ongoing reflection 153–5
  opportunity creation 120, 123,
    128
  public messages 71
  re-imagining 54
  revitalising thinking 42
  talking about emotions 113
representation 68–70
representative participation 126
research techniques
  action research 153–5
  analysis and interpretation 108
  asking questions 108
  children as researchers 108–9
  co-operation 107–8
  consent 104
  ethics 103–5
  partnership 107–8
  questions 105–7
  resource sheet 168
researchers, children as 108–9
resource sheets
  assessing opportunities 169–70
  giving it a go 171
  image of the child 164–7
  impact ripple effect 154–5, 174
  learning 173
  project review 172
  research techniques 168
resources 175–6
review planning 67–70
revitalising thinking 25–6
  assumptions 29ff
  defining noise 28
  detox 27ff
  future child 35–9
  future child to active child 51
  image and practice 45–7
  image of the child 42–5
  imagining difference 53–4
  noticing children's experience
    47–9

practice of others 46–8
protected child 39–42
protected child to participating
  child 52
recognising noise 27–9, 30
reflections and conclusions 161
refreshing image of children
  49–53
  universal child 30–5
  universal child to individual child
    50
rhetoric to reality 83–4
*Richard Cardinal: Cry from the diary of a
  Métis Child* (Obomsawin) 78
rights
  language of 93–6
  and participation 62–3
ripple model 154–5, 174
Roberts-Holmes, G. 103
Robin Hood effect 33–4
Robinson, K. 15, 142
Rooke, A. 120
Rotherham abuse case 58–9

Sarason, S.B. 68
Save the Children 96, 152
Savyasaachi 92
school-based approach 19
school council 69–70
school strikes 116–17
schools
  children's voices 53
  learning opportunities 86–7
Schwab, M. 97
Scraton, P. 32
self confidence 118
self esteem 119
self respect 119
Shier, Harry 98–100
Shier's model 98–100
60s scoop 77–8
slavery 36–7
social agent, child as 64
social change, 1800s 40
socialisation theory 17

solutions
  identifying 158
  using 159
South Africa
  community empowerment 135–8
  language 92–3
spaces, experiencing 13
spatial awareness
  activities and practices 67–8
  conclusions 76
  continuing research 75
  development framework 59–60
  focus groups 71–5
  language and tone 67
  motivation 60–1
  overview 55–6
  public messages 70–1
  reflections and conclusions 161–2
  representation 68–70
  review criteria 60–6
  review planning 67–70
  starting conversation 70–5
  views of children 56–7
speaking and listening 101
starting points 154
steps 20–1
stimulus and response 16
subject, child as 64

talking
  creating change 145–6
  and listening 157
teachers, attitudes to children 68
technical vocabulary
  defining participation 92–3
  Hart's model 96–8
  language of rights 93–6
  overview 91–2

Shier's model 98–100
thinking, influences on 27–8
transformation, thinking about 130
transformational participation 126–7

Unicef, Child Friendly Cities project 51
United Nations Convention on the Rights of the Child (UNCRC) 1989 39, 62, 78, 93–6
universal child 30–5
  to individual child 50
Urinboyev, R. 53
US Declaration of Independence 35

values 11
visibility 69–70
voices
  creating platforms for 115
  and exercise of power 52–3
  modes of hearing 16
  valuing 69–70
voting age 52
voting rights 39

Washington, George 34–5
water patterns, as emotional categories 111
White, S. 126
William, Prince 26
Wollstonecraft, Mary 37
women, and competence 37–9

Yousefzi, Malala 15–16, 122

Sam Frankel is Creative Director of EquippingKids. Sam has spent over 15 years dedicated to promoting understanding of children's everyday lives. His work combines both an academic and practical engagement with children and their place at home, school and in the community. Sam is an Honorary Research Fellow at the University of Sheffield and has recently spent two years as a Visiting Professor at King's University College at the University of Western Ontario, Canada. Sam has worked with tens of thousands of children across the UK. His research and ideas are shared in a growing number of publications.